ALSO BY CANDACE SAVAGE

SCIENCE AND NATURE
Prairie: A Natural History
Mother Nature: Animal Parents and Their Young
The Nature of Wolves: An Intimate Portrait
Bird Brains: The Intelligence of Crows, Ravens, Magpies and Jays
Aurora: The Mysterious Northern Lights
Wild Cats
Peregrine Falcons
Grizzly Bears
Wolves
Eagles of North America
The Wonder of Canadian Birds
(published in the U.S. as *Wings of the North*)
Wild Mammals of Western Canada
(published in the U.S. as *Wild Mammals of Northwest
America*; coauthor with Arthur Savage)

CULTURAL HISTORY
Witch: The Wild Ride from Wicked to Wicca
Beauty Queens
Cowgirls
Our Nell: A Scrapbook Biography of Nellie L. McClung
A Harvest Yet to Reap: A History of Prairie Women

FOR CHILDREN
Wizards: An Amazing Journey through the Last Great Age of Magic
Born to Be a Cowgirl: A Spirited Ride through the Old West
Eat Up! Healthy Food for a Healthy Earth
Get Growing! How the Earth Feeds Us
Trash Attack! Garbage and What We Can Do About It

ONE WOMAN'S EXPLORATION

OF THE NATURAL WORLD

CANDACE SAVAGE

CURIOUS
by Nature

GREYSTONE BOOKS

DOUGLAS & McINTYRE PUBLISHING GROUP

VANCOUVER/TORONTO/BERKELEY

Greystone Books
A division of Douglas & McIntyre Ltd.
2323 Quebec Street, Suite 201
Vancouver, British Columbia
Canada V5T 4S7

Library and Archives Canada Cataloguing in Publication
Savage, Candace, date
Curious by nature : one woman's exploration of the
natural world / Candace Savage.
Includes bibliographical references and index.

ISBN 1-55365-092-1

1. Natural history. 2. Human ecology. 3. Nature. I. Title.
QH81.S28 2005   508   C2005-900018-x

Library of Congress Cataloging-in-Publication Data
Savage, Candace, date.
Curious by nature : one woman's exploration of the
natural world / Candace Savage.
p. cm.
Includes bibliographical references (p.).
ISBN 1-55365-092-1 (trade paper : alk. paper)
1. Animals—North America. 2. Natural History—North America. I. Title.
QL151.S38 2005
508.7—dc22   2004060851

Editing by Jane Billinghurst
Copy editing by Viola Funk
Cover and text design by Jessica Sullivan
Cover image by Walter Bibikow / Getty Images
Printed and bound in Canada by Friesens
Printed on acid-free paper that is forest friendly
(100% post-consumer recycled paper) and has been processed chlorine-free
Distributed in the U.S. by Publishers Group West

We gratefully acknowledge the financial support of the Canada Council for the Arts,
the British Columbia Arts Council, and the Government of Canada through the Book
Publishing Industry Development Program (BPIDP) for our publishing activities.

CONTENTS

Going Wild

One of the best things that ever happened to me was being stung by a bee. I was only two or three years old at the time, and my memory of the event has blurred around the margins, like an old-fashioned photograph. Somewhere, grayed back into the distance, lies the big, wood-frame house where I lived with my family. But neither my mother nor my father nor my sister is with me. I am all alone in a wide expanse of grass, and a yellow-and-black bee is walking on my hand. Already, I have watched as it crept, glistening, from my elbow, up my forearm, and onto my palm. I have never in all my life seen anything so beautiful. My small body is alight with wonder.

A moment later, disaster strikes and I run screaming into the house. How could anything so pretty have hurt me so much? Yet fifty years on, I've begun to think of that brief trauma as a lasting gift. The flash of pain had etched the bee—

in all its glory—onto my memory. Though I can no longer recapture the sensation of seeing the world with new eyes, I can at least remember a time when I remembered it.

Since then, innocence has given way to experience, and I am no longer able to consider every insect with the respect it deserves. The joyful shock of the Very First Time cannot be repeated. But I still get a buzz of delight every time I find out something new or revisit a familiar experience or fact from a fresh perspective. Learning gives me pleasure, even when it carries a sting. And it is that satisfaction—the pure, animal happiness of sniffing around and finding something worth chewing on—that I hope to share with you through this collection of writings.

The essays assembled in these pages were written over a period of twenty years, between 1985 and 2005. (A complete list of the sources from which they were drawn appears at the end of the book. In preparing the material for re-publication, I have updated facts and figures and reported on recent events to bring the stories up to the present.) The earliest entry in the collection, "Storm-Petrels: At Home with the Tubenoses," originally appeared in a book published in Canada as *The Wonder of Canadian Birds* and in the United States as *Wings of the North*. One of seventy short species accounts that make up that volume, the piece included here focuses on unexpected aspects of the storm-petrels' reproductive and family behavior. This theme is not surprising, given that at the time it was written, I was newly widowed and playing a harried mother hen to my then two-year-old daughter, Diana. Much of the writing for *Birds/Wings* was done during nursery-school classes and the half-hour respite offered by the children's television series *Mr. Dressup!*

Over the next decade or so, my life flowed around many an unexpected bend, sweeping me, and Diana along with me, from Saskatoon, Saskatchewan—the Paris of the Prairies—to Edmonton, Alberta, with its family connections, and then north to Yellowknife, Northwest Territories, on the shore of Great Slave Lake. My seven-year sojourn on the bedrock of the subarctic wilderness provided the setting for many adventures, some of which are recounted in these pages. I'm reminded, for example, of a once-in-a-lifetime excursion to watch a family of wolves at their den on the tundra and of the heart-stopping moment when I found myself dumped out on a barren esker, somewhere in the High Arctic, while a research team in a helicopter attempted to capture a grizzly bear on the other side of the ridge! (I am relieved to report that they tranquilized the bear and then returned to collect me.) Essays like "The Nature of Wolves: Wild Lives" and "A Future for Grizzlies: Artemis Beckons" were inspired by moments like these, when I was privileged to sense the electric vitality of living things.

Meanwhile, there was also a quieter drama unfolding during those northern years as I—a thirty-something single parent with a full-time job, a waggish, freckle-faced daughter, and an ever-growing menagerie of silly pets—began to get my bearings as a writer. Morning after morning, I discovered myself crawling out of bed in the cold and dark, so that I could fit in a couple of hours of writing before regular school-and-work hours. No one was more surprised than I by this weird behavior. But if I was prepared to give up the comforts of sleep in order to hunch over a computer keyboard, then my desire to learn and to write deserved to be acknowledged. The job and the pay check would have to go and, with them, the high costs of living in the North. If I intended to work as a writer, it was time to move on.

And so the early 1990s brought me and my chancy aspirations back to where I had begun, on the Great Plains grasslands. A stubble-jumper by breeding and inclination, I was raised in the Peace River country of northwestern Alberta, educated at the University of Alberta in Edmonton, and, for the past decade, have found myself most at home in the wide open spaces of Saskatchewan. Despite a population density on a par with that of Mongolia, my adopted province boasts a rich artistic community and a standard of cultural services—including the first arts board on the continent—that have supported my quixotic ambition to earn my living as a writer. And if the magnetic pull of the North helped me to find my course, the generosity of the prairies has encouraged me to put down roots. A deepening appreciation for the prairie ecosystem—and an opportunity for uninterrupted periods of research and reflection now that my chick has flown from the nest—are reflected in the most recent writings in this collection: "Prairyerths: Entering the Underworld" and "Stuck on the Prairies: Where Is Here?", both of which are excerpted from *Prairie: A Natural History*, published in 2004, and "Dances with Bison: The Wild and the Tame," which appeared in *Canadian Geographic* magazine in January/February 2005.

Over the years, I've written about everything from A to Z, from the astrophysics of the northern lights to the devious zoology of parasites. The thread that ties all these explorations together is my curiosity about the natural world. Yet, strange as it may seem, I have never thought of myself as a "nature writer." For better or for worse, I have been blessed with a short concentration span and a mind that constantly flits outside the bounds of a narrowly defined genre. During the period when the works in this collection were created, I also wrote books for children and adults on such subjects as garbage, agriculture, nutrition, cowgirls, beauty contests, witches, and the practice of magic in early-modern Europe. I flatter myself that I have a magpie mind, always alert, always on the lookout for something worth checking out. But no matter what subject I'm addressing, my goal has always been the same: to write accurately and with feeling about real things, organisms, people and events, and to honor the magic of language.

Quite apart from a desire for broad horizons, my discomfort with the idea of "nature writing" also has a deeper source. By my reading at least, most so-called nature writing is not primarily about nature. Many respected writers—more power to their pens—use their encounters with non-human nature as a backdrop for meditations on human existence. In this, they are following in the exalted footsteps of philosopher-poets like Ralph Waldo Emerson and Henry David Thoreau, for whom the facts of nature were not merely phenomena but signs and symbols of transcendence. The philosophical interpretation of nature is a high calling, but it has not been my path. Instead, my intention has been both humbler and perhaps less achievable: to bring the ungraspable reality of the non-human world into clearer focus. Even as you read these words, the wild world is out there.

In my attempt to make wild lives tangible and to bring them into our everyday awareness, I have been drawn into a love-hate relationship with science. Except for the senior zoology classes that I crammed into my English degree, I have no formal training in any scientific or technical specialty. Yet in the course of preparing these essays, I have read literally thousands of scientific papers and had the pleasure of consulting with dozens of scientists, often the leading researchers in their fields of study. The contrast between the animation—even passion—

of these extraordinary people and the meticulously worded tedium of their published reports has never ceased to cause me mild alarm. It is hard to quarrel with a scientific methodology that can range from the soil to the sea to the stars with triumphant ease, answering questions and resolving mysteries. But at the same time, there is surely something worrying about a tradition that requires its practitioners to present themselves in print as number-crunching machines, devoid of hopes, fears, ambitions, and the occasional wild-eyed theory. In writing about the findings of natural science, I have tried to put the flesh of emotion back onto the bare bones of fact and to convey current, accurate information in a meaningful, real-life context.

That context has not always been pleasant. In preparing these essays, I have repeatedly been forced to confront the destruction that we, as high-end consumers of the world's splendor, are leaving in our wake. In a world where the wonder of life is slowly blinking out all around us, it is no doubt important to raise the alarm. But despair is a bleak and sullen emotion and cannot be an end in itself. Once stung into action, we need the lift of a hopeful vision to buoy us up: the knowledge that life can, and often does, change for the better. To reword Pogo's famous dictum, we have seen the answer, and it is us. The journey forward begins in amazement.

THIS COLLECTION would not have been possible without my long and pleasurable friendship with Rob Sanders of Greystone Books and a more recent, but equally fruitful, relationship with Rick Boychuk at *Canadian Geographic* magazine. The anthology took shape under the skilled and speedy direction of Jane Billinghurst, who not only selected the articles and excerpts included here but also helped to oversee the production of the book. In addition, appreciation is due to Shelley Tanaka and Nancy Flight of Greystone Books and to Sylvia Barrett and Eric Harris of *Canadian Geographic*, each of whom brought their talents to one or another of these texts at the time of first publication.

Among the experts who generously shared their time and knowledge in the preparation of these essays are: Ralph Archibald, British Columbia Ministry of Environment; Larry Aumiller and Rob Boertje, Alaska Department of Fish and Game; George Blondin, Dene Cultural Institute; Peter Butala, Old Man on His Back Prairie and Heritage Conservation Area; Tom J. Cade, World Center for Birds of Prey; Peter Clarkson, Doug Heard, Mitch Taylor, and Mark Williams, Northwest Territories Department of Renewable Resources; Stan Cuthand, Elder, Saskatoon; David Ellis, Institute for Raptor Studies; Cormack Gates, University of Calgary; John Gunson, Alberta Forestry, Lands and Wildlife; Stephen Herrero, Eastern Slope Grizzly Bear Study; Martin Jalkotzy and the late Ian Ross, Alberta Cougar Project; Sam James, Department of Biology, Maharishi University of Management; Scott Jarvie, City of Toronto; Dan Johnson, University of Lethbridge; Murdoch McAllister, Simon Fraser University; Wayne McCrory, McCrory Wildlife Services; Mary Ann McLean, Indiana State University; Bruce McLellan and Tony Hamilton, British Columbia Ministry of the Environment; L. David Mech, United States Geological Survey; Marshall Patterson, Saskatchewan Bison Association; Don Russell, Doug Forsyth, and Pierre Mineau, Canadian Wildlife Service; Christopher Servheen, University of Montana; Douglas Smith and Dan Stahler, Yellowstone National Park; Paddy Thompson and Lyn Oliphant, University of Saskatchewan; and James C. Trager, Shaw Nature Reserve,

Missouri. Sincere thanks are owed to each of these people and to the dozens of other researchers to whom I have spoken over the years. If despite all the expert advice I've been given, there are errors in these texts, they are entirely my own responsibility.

Finally, it is a special pleasure to acknowledge the support of my daughter, Diana Savage, who grew up with these projects and—in spite of watching me struggle to learn my craft and listening to me complain—has gone on to become a skilled writer in her own right. Thanks beyond measure are also due to Keith Bell, my companion in all things, for a shared love of exploring.

SURPRISING

Lives

PARASITES

Nature's Cling-Ons

Of all nature's creations, few are less appealing to humans than parasites. Yet get past the initial disgust and these lowly creatures begin to exert a perverse fascination. They even demand a grudging respect for the ingenuity with which they conspire against their hosts.

Take, for example, a humble worm known as the lancet fluke. Like many parasites, it passes through several stages in the course of its life, each of which requires a different host. At one juncture, the fluke must pass directly from the body of an ant into a sheep—a transition that would be a lot simpler if the two species ordinarily met. But ants generally stay near the ground, while sheep browse on the tips of vegetation. The fluke overcomes this difficulty by invading the ant in the form of larvae, which infest the nervous system. Under this foreign control, the ant suddenly and unaccountably decides to climb a tall blade of grass and lock its jaws shut on the tip. Unable to escape the lancet fluke's command, the ant has no choice but to await its ovine nemesis.

This bizarre plot was unraveled almost forty years ago by Wilhelm Hohorst and colleagues in Frankfurt, Germany. Parasites, it seems, were not just unwelcome passengers in their hosts' bodies; they were a potent force with an unexpected impact on ecological networks. Who had ever heard of a sheep that ate ants?

Since then, dozens of quirky variations on this alien-invasion theme have been documented by parasitologists. In the early 1970s, for example, William Bethel and John Holmes of the University of Alberta studied the behavior of small aquatic crustaceans called amphipods. Healthy amphipods, they discovered, prefer to stay near the bottom of ponds, where they are relatively safe from predators. But if they become infected with *Polymorphus paradoxus,* a parasitic worm, they begin to seek the bright lights of the surface. This increases their chances of being eaten by surface-feeders like mallards, muskrats, and beavers—the very species within which *P. paradoxus* must complete its life cycle. Amphipods infested with a different worm, *P. marilis,* are drawn only part way up, into the realm of that parasite's ultimate hosts, the diving ducks. And so it goes.

Even plants can be subject to hostile takeovers. Blueberries (both wild and cultivated) are afflicted by a disease called "mummy berry," which is caused by a fungus. The first symptoms appear in spring, when tender young leaves are infected by wind-borne spores. The foliage droops and turns brown and the leaves become coated with spores. As unappealing as they are to human eyes, the leaves now attract insects, which crawl over the discolored surfaces and feed intently. Under the influence of the disease, the foliage has suddenly begun to produce sugars. What's more, the leaves have also developed ultra-violet markings—visible to insects—which mimic the "nectar-guides" on blueberry blossoms.

When the insects bumble off to visit the plant's real flowers, they deposit mummy-berry spores (picked up from the leaves) on the stigmas. As a result of this infection, the blueberry plant produces shriveled, infertile fruit, within which the fungus survives the winter, ready to resume its dirty tricks next spring.

Only occasionally are victims able to shift the balance of power and defend their own interests. For example, bumble-bees parasitized by the conopid fly often choose to spend nights out in the cold rather than seek shelter within the communal nest. By letting their bodies cool, they slow the parasite's growth and may prevent it from maturing before their own, natural deaths. Recent research by Murdoch McAllister and colleagues at Simon Fraser University in Burnaby, British Columbia, suggests that pea aphids infected by wasps commit suicide to protect close relatives from coming in contact with the parasite. Death by desiccation—dropping to the parched earth—seems to be their preferred means of self-sacrifice.

Parasites are opportunists, with a cool, criminal disregard for the integrity of their victims. "What's mine is mine and what's yours is mine" might be their motto. But far from being an ecological offense, this is the way of a world in which lives interpenetrate each other. Working from the inside to complicate and subvert natural relationships, parasites are hackers in the worldwide web of life.

A GREAT DAY
FOR GRASSHOPPERS

Outings in Entomology

an Johnson holds 50 million years of evolution between his forefinger and thumb. "It's *Psoloessa delicatula,* the brown-spotted range grasshopper," he says. "A female. See?" The entomologist upends the small, delicately barred insect and gently squeezes its abdomen until four dark prongs poke out. "She uses those to dig herself into the ground when she lays her eggs . . . she buries them wrapped in foam.

"What a little gem," he says as he watches the insect whirl away from his hand. "I didn't expect it to be so good out here. This is a great day for grasshoppers!"

Johnson is one of North America's leading experts on the ecology and control of grasshoppers. A youthful forty-something, with a runner's lean build, he moves across the pasture with birdlike energy, his large white net flapping at the end of a long handle. From a distance, he looks like a child chasing butterflies. If good science is mostly play disguised as work, as biologist E.O. Wilson once said, this has all the hallmarks of good science.

Today's field trip has brought us half an hour west of Lethbridge, Alberta (where Johnson, until recently a research scientist with Agriculture and Agri-Foods Canada, is now a professor of environmental science), to a scrubby expanse of native grassland, splatted with cowpies and frazzled by the sun. As we step across the close-cropped thatch of blue grama and needle-and-thread grass, grasshoppers spurt away from our feet in silver arcs. To the untutored eye, they are mere blurs of motion, but to Johnson, these brief sightings are vivid with detail.

"Did you see that?" he says, his face alight with delight. "A male *Arphia conspersa,* the speckled rangeland grasshopper, with the blood-red wings. And look at that *Eritettix simplex.* Did you see its body? Bright lime-green. That is a beautiful grasshopper."

A beautiful grasshopper? Don't let them catch you saying that downtown on coffee row! To generations of prairie farmers and ranchers, grasshoppers have looked like nothing but trouble, ugly little chewing machines whose mouthparts are perfectly adapted to take a bite out of the bottom line. Where is the beauty in creatures that can cut through pastures and croplands like a biblical plague until, as the book of Exodus puts it, "not a green thing" remains?

Johnson has no illusions about the damage that grasshoppers can do. Yet for him they are not merely pests. They are also small morsels of life, as lovely in their own way as birds, and a vital component of grassland ecosystems. And that is why he has devoted his life to improving pest-control techniques and to telling a doubting world that even the despised grasshopper deserves our care and concern.

ON THE FRONT LINES

Up until two hundred years ago, two major herbivores dominated the Great Plains. One was the bison; the other was the Rocky Mountain locust, *Melanoplus spretus.* (Locusts are grasshoppers that periodically erupt in swarms.) In the 1870s, plagues of locusts advanced across the plains, stripping bare thousands of sections of cropland and native grasses. Dark clouds of the insects filled the air and cast an eerie twilight over the landscape. One huge swarm was estimated to extend over the area of eleven states. To this day, there are layers of locust bodies trapped where they landed in the ice of Grasshopper Glacier in south-central Montana, a visible reminder of historic outbreaks.

By the early 1900s, the voracious hordes of locusts had inexplicably vanished, plunging from superabundance to apparent extinction in less than three decades. (In his book *Prairie Soul,* published in 2004, Jeffrey Lockwood, the reigning expert on the Rocky Mountain locust, hints that a remnant population may be clinging to existence in Yellowstone National Park.) Although nobody knows why the population crashed as it did, scientists surmise that the locusts were undone by some combination of natural and human-induced causes. For example, the planting of alfalfa may have weakened them, since grasshoppers don't grow well on it. Cultivation, livestock grazing, irrigation, and introduced bird species may also have contributed to their demise.

But far from solving farmers' problems, the locusts' disappearance merely opened the way for other malefactors to emerge, including the lesser migratory, the clear-winged, the two-striped, the Packard's, and two or three other species of grasshoppers. These are the insects that devastated the Great

Plains during the droughts of the Dirty Thirties. Nothing was safe from their shearing mandibles, not even laundry hanging on the line. And these same species are still significant agricultural pests, taking more than U.S.$75 million, by Johnson's estimate, from the pockets of prairie farmers during an average infestation year.

From first-hand experience, Johnson appreciates the losses inflicted by a major infestation. He arrived in Lethbridge in 1983, just in time to witness the buildup to the most serious grasshopper outbreak on the prairies in recent decades. A series of dry, warm years had increased grasshopper reproduction and survival and created unfavorable conditions for fungi and other infectious agents that attack grasshopper nymphs: in other words, perfect conditions for the hoppers to breed and survive and breed again.

"That first fall, I predicted a fourfold increase in grasshoppers for the next year," says Johnson, "but management wasn't sure I was right, because I was just a young guy and no one else was calling for such a big jump." But the young guy was right, and he was right again the following year, when the population surged ahead by another 500 percent. Out on the front lines, the situation quickly degenerated from a problem into a crisis. Farm-supply stores hadn't ordered enough insecticide to meet the explosive demand, and the armed forces had to be called in to airlift emergency supplies.

In 1985, as the infestation peaked, farmers and commercial applicators sprayed some 4 million hectares (nearly 10 million acres) across the three Canadian prairie provinces—a treatment area more than twice the size of Lake Ontario. Over 400,000 liters, or quarts, of insecticide were applied in Alberta alone, a bombardment that affected not only the pest species but also insect predators, such as some flies and beetles that could have provided a measure of natural control. Carbofuran, a widely used application, proved toxic to birds, including several dozen California gulls that died after feeding on poisoned grasshoppers in Saskatchewan. It was subsequently taken off the market as a grasshopper-control agent.

Amid this calamity, Johnson found the focus for the rest of his career. "Our job is not just to control grasshoppers," he realized. "We have to control them responsibly." Instead of clubbing the ecosystem into submission, Johnson saw the need to approach the problem with insight and delicacy. He sensed that this would be possible only by appreciating the subtleties of prairie ecosystems and the complex roles of the insects within them. It was time to get up close and personal with grasshoppers.

SNAKES IN THE COUCH

Since his boyhood on the plains of South Dakota, Johnson had been preparing for this calling. A science bug even then, he kept the house hopping with frogs, whirring with mayflies, and squirming with leeches. Once, memorably, a stash of garter snakes emerged from the living room couch. He had an insect collection and a notebook filled with meticulous drawings of aquatic organisms.

Childhood friend Joe Nadenicek, now ombudsman for small business with the Department of Environment and Natural Resources in South Dakota, remembers the long, happy summer days he and Johnson spent poking along the shores of Marne Creek. "I was just kicking the dirt," Nadenicek jokes, "but Dan had a real affinity for fish and bugs—finding them, examining them, noticing the habitats they came from. He was definitely a born naturalist."

It was a passion that seemed to have come from nowhere, an interest that was not shared with parents or friends. "It was basically something I did by myself," Johnson says. Then a chance encounter with a college biology student opened his eyes to a new world of possibility. Grownups could care about insects; a childhood fascination can turn into a lifelong pursuit.

A brief adolescent lapse of concentration saw Johnson graduate from high school without a single science or math credit. "I worked at a furniture factory in Saskatoon, making chairs and couches for two dollars an hour, and was happy doing it," he says. "When I decided to quit and go to university, I had to take grade-12 science and math at night while starting first year."

Johnson eventually earned a high-honors degree in biology from the University of Saskatchewan in Saskatoon. His doctoral work at the University of British Columbia in Vancouver focused on the ecology of mites in apple orchards. "Like studying angels on the heads of pins," he says. While doing so, he honed two skills that would form the basis of his grasshopper research: detailed field observation and sophisticated computer modeling.

Johnson began his grassland studies with the assumption that grasshoppers had not evolved simply to plague farmers and ranchers. "These animals have the grasslands written right into them," he says. "They are grassland symbols."

A SQUIRT IN TIME

Only a handful of the hundred or so grasshopper species found on the prairies ever graze heavily enough to become agricultural pests. Many, such as the lovely little brown-spotted range grasshopper that we met on our field trip, have no direct economic significance but hold a central place in the food webs of the Great Plains.

Unlike most grasshoppers, which lay eggs in July and August and hatch out in early June, brown-spotted range grasshoppers hatch in midsummer and overwinter as miniature nymphs. In the spring, these immature forms quickly metamorphose into adults, which appear just in time to serve as baby food for songbird nestlings. For example, a study conducted by Johnson and colleagues from the Canadian Wildlife Service in 1995 found that grasshoppers comprised more than 85 percent of the food brought to nests of chestnut-collared longspurs, *Calcarius ornatus*, a common grassland bird. Of these, a high percentage were the conveniently bite-sized brown-spotted range grasshoppers.

"I've been on a campaign to get people to leave this species alone," Johnson says. "I think it should be protected." He feels the same way about the red-winged and club-horned grasshoppers and a couple of other early-season species favored by birds. "I've talked to farm groups until I'm hoarse," Johnson says emphatically. "The grasshoppers you see in May are not pests; there is never a need to spray them."

To their credit, farmers and ranchers have been responsive. Johnson recalls a spring day a few years ago when he stopped at a community pasture to check for grasshoppers. A rancher pulled up in his pickup and came over to chat. "You don't have to worry about those grasshoppers with the colored wings, the ones you see in May," the man told him. "I've heard they never cause problems." It turned out the rancher had recently heard Johnson interviewed on the radio.

"I think farmers and ranchers are relieved to know when they can safely do nothing," Johnson says. But they also need to know when and where to take decisive action, and he is happy to offer some useful pointers. Since the potential pest species hatch out in late May or early June (depending on the temperature), this is a critical period for vigilance. If, at that time, a farmer detects more than ten grasshoppers in a square meter, or yard, together with significant damage to crops, the situation is heading into the danger zone. By "spot treating" infested areas early in the growing season, it may be possible to avoid large-scale outbreaks as the crops mature. "Spraying five hectares (a dozen or so acres) early," says Johnson, "could save hundreds later on."

This philosophy—that a squirt in time may save nine— also provided the motivation for Johnson's pioneering use of geographic information systems (GIS), computer programs combining survey data with such variables as soil, temperature, and precipitation to make maps that forecast grasshopper outbreaks in the prairie provinces. Johnson has produced GIS forecasts annually since 1987. Grasshopper counts conducted each August at four thousand locations across the prairies are combined with relevant environmental data, worked up on the computer, and published on the Internet as a colorful, easy-to-read map.

"It's pretty simple," Johnson says. "If the grasshoppers are there in August, the eggs will be there in the spring." But this simple system has proven so valuable that it has become a model for monitoring insect pests across the Canadian prairies and in other parts of the world. Johnson's forecasts give a heads-up to farmers and ranchers about where severe infestations are likely to develop, allowing them to focus their efforts and ultimately reduce the amount of pesticide used. The goal is to maximize economic benefit and minimize environmental risk, and Johnson is justifiably proud of his contribution to improving this balance.

"We're searching so hard for environmentally sustainable approaches to pest control," says Lloyd Dosdall, an agricultural entomologist with the University of Alberta in Edmonton. "Dan is at the forefront of all that research. He's a resource person not just here in North America but worldwide, particularly in the use of GIS to predict insect outbreaks." Dosdall says he is especially impressed by Johnson's ability to manipulate complicated mathematical modeling systems and translate the information into language any layperson can understand. "That's a real gift," he adds.

Over the years, the regard of colleagues has been expressed in numerous honors paid to Johnson, including an award from the Entomological Society of Canada in 1992 for "research achievements and service by an individual under 40" and, more recently, a team gold medal from the government of Canada for distinguished research.

Yet Johnson has a nagging feeling that something is still amiss. "We could do better," he says.

CHANGING EXPECTATIONS

The insecticides currently on the market are blunt instruments capable of harming any insect they come in contact with. Unlike the organochlorines of old, none of them persist for long in the environment, but some (including chlorpyrifos, which was recently pulled from the U.S. market but is still licensed for use as a hopper-control agent in Canada) are toxic to warm-blooded creatures. Others, such as the pyrethroids deltamethrin and lambda-cyhalothrin, are safe for birds and mammals but harmful to fish, amphibians, and aquatic invertebrates. None is without a measure of risk.

Johnson looks forward to the day when we can hit the target bang on, using biological controls or chemicals that attack specific species or groups. Could we, for example, deploy microorganisms that cause epidemics exclusively among pest species of grasshoppers? So far, four such organisms (three fungi and a protozoan) hold promise. Unlike a chemical pesticide that acts on contact, these agents may take a week or more to get going and do not always result in death. "You have to wait, take your time," Johnson says. "You need to lower your expectations about them dropping dead."

But if the goal is to suppress the population below the threshold at which it can cause economic losses (rather than wipe it out), these agents have something to offer. One of the disease-causing fungi was recently approved for use against locusts in Madagascar, thanks in part to research by Johnson and his collaborator, Judit Smits of the Toxicology Centre at the University of Saskatchewan. Applications to register two of the organisms in Canada were rejected ten years ago, but recent changes in the regulations appear to have opened a new avenue of hope.

The need for these alternatives is growing. A severe and spreading drought on the prairies over the past several years has raised the alarm about a renewed grasshopper crisis in the near future. Grasshopper populations rise and fall with the weather. A cool, rainy spring brings on disease and sends hopper numbers crashing down. But when the rains fail—as they eventually will—a renewed grasshopper emergency becomes inevitable.

Farmers and ranchers will face future onslaughts with fewer weapons than they had during the outbreak of the mid-1980s, thanks to the withdrawal of Carbofuran in Canada and restrictions on chlorpyrifos in the United States. As awareness of the environmental impact of pesticides grows, Johnson sees the possibility that other broad-spectrum insecticides will be taken off the market. "I think it's inevitable that products with unintended impacts will be removed or restricted," he says.

We can face this challenge now, as a matter of principle, or later, out of necessity. In Johnson's view, it is high time for us to get hopping.

PRAIRYERTHS

Entering the Underworld

*T*he soil has been described as the "poor person's tropical rainforest," one of the richest and most diverse ecosystems anywhere on Earth. And nowhere is this more obvious than on the Great Plains. Recent estimates suggest that the total weight, or biomass, of all the invisible organisms that live in prairie soils is greater than the mass of all the visible, above-ground animals put together. If all the microflora and micro-fauna from grassland soils could be piled onto one arm of some Great Cosmic Scale, with all the reptiles, mammals, and birds from the upper world heaped onto the other pan, the balance would tip sharply toward the soil organisms. Together with the plant roots around which they live, these little creatures are the powerhouse of the prairie, responsible for anywhere between 60 and 90 percent of all the biological activity on the Great Plains.

The most numerous organisms in this busy world are also the smallest—thousands upon thousands of different kinds of single-celled organisms, including algae, fungi, bacteria, and protozoans. Although a few of these creatures may be familiar from Biology 101—the ooze-along, blob-shaped amoebae, for example, and the whip-tailed flagellates—many (if not most) of the soil microbes are still completely unknown, never having been studied, named, or even seen by anyone. A single teaspoon of dirt typically holds around 5 billion of these fantastically varied little animals and plants, all of them fiercely engaged in the business of life and death. In their billions and their trillions, they expend as much energy as if several thousand people were living on every acre of the prairies.

Adding to the hubbub is a lively assemblage of somewhat larger (though still mostly microscopic) and more complex animals. The bestiary includes plump, lumbering, eight-legged little critters called tardigrades, or waterbears, that waddle through the film of water around soil granules, searching for food. When they find plant roots or fungi, the "bears" drill into the cells with their sharp snouts, or stylets, and suck out the nourishing fluids. Another, more important group of plant eaters, the springtails, spend their lives bumbling blindly through the dirt, munching on bacteria, fungi, dying roots, and the occasional dead waterbear or worm. Jumpy and alert, springtails are equipped to leap into action at the first tremor of danger. As their name suggests, they have spring-loaded tails that when all is well they carry tucked up under their abdomens. But when danger is detected, the tail fills with fluid and suddenly snaps down, sending the springtail catapulting to what, with luck, is safer ground. (The light-colored specks of "dust" that sometimes somersault away from compost when the pile is turned are actually springtails taking flight from the disturbance.)

One square meter of prairie can support anywhere from 5,000 to 15,000 springtails in the top thirty centimeters of soil. (That's about a square yard dug to the depth of a foot, or enough to make a couple of wheelbarrow loads.) But these statistics pale compared with the totals for another major group of soil dwellers. The soil is crawling with microscopic mites, those scurrying, scuttling, eight-legged cousins of spiders and ticks. The same small patch of prairie soil that is hopping with springtails may simultaneously be home to up to 60,000 mites, representing dozens, or even hundreds, of species. (Although 48,000 kinds of mites have so far been identified around the world, the final catalog of species is expected to reach half a million or more.) While many mites make their living peaceably by feeding on microbes and plant roots, others are voracious predators—the tigers of this invisible world. *Spinibdella cronini,* for example, is a largish red mite (about the size of the period at the end of this sentence) that is common in prairie soils and that preys on soft-bodied mites and springtails. Its modus operandi is to seize its prey by surprise, tie it down with silk, and then suck the life out of it.

Pity the poor springtails. For "giant" mites are not the only menace in their shadowy world. They must also be prepared to flee from pseudoscorpions, jaunty little monsters that stalk through the soil with their venomous pincers armed and ready for action. Danger can also come swimming through the darkness in the form of carnivorous worms, innocuous-looking creatures (mostly smaller than the letter *i*) that either swallow their prey whole or attach themselves to the victim's body and scrape at it until the internal organs can be drawn out through the puncture. These silent predators are members of an enormous tribe of roundworms, or nematodes, that are the most numerous multicellular animals on the grasslands. Hundreds of species have been found at sites across the Great Plains, including those that feed on bacteria, protozoans, fungi, algae, mites, other nematodes, and the roots of higher plants, or some combination of the above. A heap of soil that contains thousands of springtails and mites typically also holds between 3 million and 5 million nematodes. Across the broad expanse of the grasslands, their numbers spin out of control, quickly mounting toward the astronomical.

GROWING SOIL

All soil is full of life, whether under prairie, forest, tundra, or desert. Yet compared with other biomes, the temperate grasslands are remarkable for the extent to which they concentrate their resources in the underworld. The reason is simple: it's safer down there. The prairie climate is grueling—too hot, too cold, too wet, too dry, too wild and variable—but go a little way beneath the surface and the environment becomes surprisingly equable. During the growing season, for instance, when the thermometer can easily spike from 10°C to 40°C (50°F to 105°F), the temperature half a meter (twenty inches) down in the soil remains pleasantly cool and virtually constant.

In a region where moisture is often the limiting factor for life, the soil also provides a buffer against drought. Long after the surface of the ground has been wicked dry by the sun and wind, the soil retains hidden reserves of moisture. Not only does water pool in the spaces, or pores, between the soil granules, but it is also glued to the surface of the particles by powerful chemical bonds. Thus, even apparently dry dirt often retains a thin film of water that is tightly bound to the soil grains. To tap this precious resource, grasses put down dense networks of thin, fibrous, probing, branching, fast-growing roots, all seeking moisture and nutrients. On average, grasses produce three or four times more roots by weight than they do leaves and stems, giving them a root-to-shoot ratio that is ten times as high as that of a forest.

The sheer volume of roots produced by prairie grasses is mind-boggling. In the mid-1930s, one determined agrologist undertook to excavate and measure all the roots produced by a small patch of tall-grass prairie in Nebraska. From half a square meter, or yard, of ground, he extracted about 250 kilometers (150 miles) of fibrous roots—enough, laid end to end, to reach from Lincoln, Nebraska, to Sioux City, Iowa. The tally included 17 kilometers (11 miles) of green needlegrass roots, 21 kilometers (13 miles) of big bluestem, 37 kilometers (23 miles) of little bluestem, and 176 kilometers (109 miles) of Kentucky bluegrass. And that was without factoring in the silvery fuzz of absorbent root hairs that coat root fibers from base to tip. In another heroic experiment, a single rye plant (the domesticated cousin of several native prairie grasses) was found to have produced 11,000 kilometers (7,000 miles) of roots and root hairs in one four-month growing season.

In nature, these root systems obviously do not strike out across the continent. Instead, they squiggle and writhe into every nook and cranny of the soil, holding the dirt together with their slender, grasping fibers. Since most prairie grasses also produce lateral rootstocks, or rhizomes, that send down roots along their length, each plant—and each clump of root-bound earth—is connected to the next and the next. As plant intertwines with plant, and roots interweave with roots, the soil becomes tightly tied together in a thick, fibrous mat—the famous prairie sod, which the settlers used for building their first homes.

For thousands of years before the settlers arrived, that same deep fabric of roots had served as the foundation of the soil ecosystem. The enormous biomass of underground plant matter, both living and dead, provides an almost inexhaustible supply of food for soil organisms. Huge populations of herbivores graze on the roots themselves, including hordes of fungi, nematodes, and springtails. Still other microorganisms feed on the rich soup of nutrients that leaks from the roots into the dirt. (Since these resources are concentrated in the rhizosphere—the soil that surrounds the root—much of the life in the soil is concentrated there as well.) In the dark underworld of the soil, everything gets eaten. The dead, the dying—even minute particles of excrement—are all on the menu for some miniature soil creature.

As a result of this endless round of digestion, organic material in the soil (principally dead roots) is first broken down and then gradually built back up into complex and relatively stable molecules known as humus. Dark brown or black, these humic substances not only give prairie soil its rich palette of tones but also contribute to its ability to support a dense tapestry of crops and native grasslands. To thrive, plants need to take in nutrients such as potassium and nitrogen (the K and N found in synthetic plant foods), which they soak up through their roots. Because these chemicals are water-soluble, they are readily leached down into the earth, beyond the depth at which the plants can reach after them. But if the nutrients are bound up in humus, they are effectively stored in the upper fifteen to thirty centimeters (six inches to one foot) of the soil. As the soil organisms eat away at the hard-to-digest humus, the stored nutrients are gradually supplied to the plants, much as if they were being freed from a time-release capsule.

Thus, prairie soils are fertile largely because—from the end of the Ice Age until the land was plowed—the native grasses have consistently produced more root fibers than the soil organisms have been able to consume. The surplus resources have collected in thick layers of dark, crumbly, humus-rich earth. (By contrast, desert soils contain little or no humus and forest soils have only a thin, upper horizon, or layer, of black dirt.) To an earlier generation of soil scientists, these remarkable grassland soils were known as "prairyerths," simply and profoundly because that is what they were.

STORM-PETRELS

At Home with the Tubenoses

*M*any a fisherman, in the heel and yaw of a storm-driven sea, has suddenly noticed a flock of dark-colored birds flitting daintily among the heaving waves. Tiny creatures, smaller than robins, they hover and glide amongst the crests, now rising, now turning, now skimming the water, as sure and light as butterflies in a field of flowers. And the fisherman pales, for here are "Mother Carey's Chickens," come to carry off the souls of drowning mariners.

These dreaded apparitions are really inoffensive storm-petrels, the smallest oceanic birds and members of the order Procellariiformes, or Tubenoses, a group that also includes the seafarers par excellence among living birds: albatrosses, fulmars, and shearwaters. They take their collective name from the peculiar form of their nostrils, which really are enclosed in tubes on the tops of their beaks. The function of this structure is not totally clear, though it may be an olfactory organ and certainly plays a role in salt excretion. Since Tubenoses spend almost their whole lives at sea, coming ashore only to breed, they seldom or never get fresh water to drink. But this poses no problem thanks to two large glands near the base of the bill, which extract salt from the bloodstream and excrete it through the tubular nostrils.

There are about ninety species of Tubenoses in the world, but only a few of them occur along North American shores. Of this handful, the best known are three species of "Carey's Chicks": Wilson's Storm-Petrel, a Southern Hemisphere species that spends its winter (our summer) in the North Atlantic; the Fork-tailed Storm-Petrel, a little-studied bird that breeds in the North Pacific; and Leach's Storm-Petrel, which nests on both the east and west coasts, from Labrador to Maine and from Alaska to the Baja Peninsula. As a group, they can immediately be recognized by their erratic, batlike flight, low over the sea. Some species dangle their feet onto the surface as they feed, giving the impression that they are walking on water. Hence the name "petrel," or "Little Peter," for the saint who is said to have walked the waves.

INSIDE THE AVIAN CITY

Their exceptional skill in flight no doubt contributed to the legend that storm-petrels incubate their eggs in midair, by carrying them underwing. As it turns out, the facts are scarcely less strange. In the case of Leach's Storm-Petrel, *Oceanadroma leucorhoa,* for example, the birds breed on remote, offshore islets, where they congregate in large colonies—from a few hundred to more than 1 million birds. In suitable terrain, there may be two or three nests for every square meter, or yard, of ground. Yet if you were to visit one of these avian cities by day, you might never suspect that the birds live there. From before dawn till after dark, they are in one of two places, either far out to sea, where they forage for zooplankton and small fish, or underground. Unlike Fork-tailed Storm-Petrels, which often nest in natural crevices, Leach's Storm-Petrels lay their eggs in burrows that they dig or renovate each spring. Most of this labor falls to the male of the pair. With pick and shovel (beak and feet), he hollows out a tunnel that may reach two meters, or yards, in length but is usually a third of that or less. Here, in a chamber at the end of the burrow, the female deposits her single egg, safe from the glare of gulls.

Among Leach's Storm-Petrels, eggs are usually laid in June and July. Incubation is extraordinarily long—six or seven weeks—and is shared equally, each parent serving a three- or four-day shift before taking to the sea to feed. (Since their feeding grounds are distant from the colony—often a hundred kilometers [sixty miles] or more—the adults have to commute between their food supply and their chick.) The shift change at the nest always occurs under cover of darkness. Indeed, prime time for birdwatching in a storm-petrel colony is about two hours after sunset on a foggy or overcast night. It is then the birds are most active, flying over the colony in ritualized pursuit and going to and from their nests. There is a crooning "churr" from thousands of underground nests, a tumult of staccato flight calls, and the occasional thump of small bodies colliding in the dark.

FOLLOW YOUR NOSE

The exact means by which storm-petrels find their nests is still unclear. In this hubbub, in the pitch dark, how do they zero in on one small burrow among so many, particularly since the entrances are tucked away inconspicuously under grass, stumps, rocks, and shrubs? Some researchers have suggested that storm-petrels might have sonar, like bats and certain cave-nesting birds, but there is no evidence for this. Others postulate that incoming birds orient themselves by exchanging calls with their mates waiting underground, and this may well occur, though it has not been conclusively shown. But we do know that storm-petrels rely to a considerable extent on their sense of smell, a sense so acute that some experts think a homing bird may follow the scent of its colony over tens or hundreds of kilometers, or miles. Once home, a Leach's Storm-Petrel will hover in the general vicinity of its nest, then circuit and hover again, until it has pinpointed the source of its own domestic odors. Down it plunges, perhaps landing slightly off target and stumbling toward its hole, tripping over obstacles that its nose can't detect.

The scents by which storm-petrels navigate derive from their "stomach oil," a clear, waxy liquid—orange-colored in the case of Leach's Storm-Petrels—with a strong, rancid smell. One function of this substance, which is produced by all the Tubenoses, is self-defense. When harassed, whether by predator or bird-bander, the bird vomits the reeking oil onto its enemy, sometimes causing temporary blindness. One species, the Giant Fulmar, also known as "the Stinker," can hit its victim from several meters, or yards, away.

Stomach oil is also important in the nutrition of the young. Rich in vitamins A and D, as well as in fat, it is the first food of a hatchling Leach's Storm-Petrel. On an irregular schedule of no more than one or two feedings a night, the youngster grows plump and round, increasing its weight sixteenfold in about five weeks. At that point, it far outweighs its parents and is therefore able to survive the next three or four weeks of its infancy, during which it is seldom fed. (Food supplies at sea decline late in the season.) Reduced to normal adult dimensions, it emerges from its burrow in October or November, exercises its wings on four or five successive nights, and flies out to sea. Already expert on its first flight, it is also innately able to locate the tropical waters on which its species spends the wintertime.

Once out of the nest, young Leach's Storm-Petrels may stay at sea for a year or more before returning to land for a few months of "sweethearting." Still immature, the birds arrive late in the breeding season, participate in aerial displays, dig burrows, and even occupy them for a while, but never produce eggs. They don't actually breed until they reach the age of four or five, but once mated, they usually return to the same burrows and the same partners year after year. The oldest known Leach's Storm-Petrel was still breeding at the age of twenty-four. Such long life spans are common among marine birds, an indication that the ocean, for all its violent moods and unmarked distances, is a gentle protector of species that are adapted to its ways.

UP CLOSE
and Personal

MOUNTAIN LIONS

Seeing Ghosts

Beep. Beep. Beep.

With his left hand, biologist Martin Jalkotzy lifts the small, boxlike radio receiver to his ear, trying to make the most of the faint squawks that it emits. With his right, he holds up what looks like an old-fashioned TV antenna and turns it through a jerky circuit. North, northwest, west . . .

We are standing at the edge of a paved highway, looking out over the broad, dark-green sweep of the Sheep River Valley in western Alberta. During the summer, this road is arush with cars of holiday-makers, many from nearby Calgary, who come to test themselves against the slopes of the Rocky Mountain foothills. But now, in late winter, the road is closed to regular traffic and the valley is hushed.

Beep. Beep. Beep.

Martin is still listening, chin slightly raised, eyes half shut. After several days as a guest of the Alberta Cougar Project, I know better than to interrupt him. Pinpointing signals from a radio-collared animal is less a science than an art, and Martin deserves his concentration. Besides, if he succeeds, I might get to see a wild mountain lion. I do my best to appear patient.

Beep. Beep.

Finally Martin lowers the receiver from his ear. "I think it's coming from up there," he says, jerking his head to indicate the gentle slope behind us. "She might be quite close." "She" is the source of the signals: an adult female mountain lion nicknamed Geisha, who for the past eight years has unwittingly sent out telltale beeps from a small radio transmitter that she wears under her chin. Guided by these insistent monotone messages, Martin and his colleagues have been able to gather information about her diet, movements, and sexual encounters. They know, for example, that early last fall she gave birth to two fluffy blue-eyed kittens. Are her youngsters with her now? There is only one way to find out.

We turn our backs to the road and follow a streambed through a border of meadows and open woods. If it weren't for Martin's frequent stops to consult his equipment, this walk would be no different from dozens of other afternoon rambles through the foothills. Overhead the sun breaks through fitfully; underfoot the snow and dry leaves crunch.

We have walked for about ten minutes when Martin, again checking his receiver, whispers, "This way," and makes a sharp right turn into the woods. The trees stand in clumps, with leads of open space that take us in like paths. It is so easy and so ordinary that I cannot believe anything exciting will happen.

Then it does. A burnished beige blur streaks out of a grove of willows and spruce, half a minute ahead. While I am trying to figure out what it was and where it went, Martin points toward the thicket. More brown shapes are moving in the darkness under the branches of a large spruce. As the animals shift around to get a look at us, we catch the flash of their amber eyes and brilliant white muzzles. Mountain lions.

A few minutes of utter silence. Then Martin motions me closer, leans back against a tree, and begins to offer a muttered commentary. "The animals in the thicket are—"

"Look, look, look," I sputter. Without a rustle of notice, one of the mountain lions has positioned itself in front of the spruce tree. It faces us head on, its big round eyes fixed on us like laser beams. We are all motionless. Then the animal bounds toward us, closing the space. At two-seconds' distance it stops and eyes us intently again.

Beside its back right heel, the tip of its tail ticks.

"It's okay," Martin whispers. "It's just curious." Sure enough, this is no snarling, ears-back, mad-cat attack. Instead the animal looks incredulous, as if confronted by aliens from outer space. Its unblinking, round-eyed stare never wavers. It bounces closer.

Martin takes a step forward. The cat turns away; another step from Martin and it scoots back to the safety of the thicket. Martin and I turn as well and walk back to the road.

About the time I start breathing again, I realize that Martin is trying to fill me in on what has happened. The animal who came toward us was one of Geisha's half-grown kittens, a youngster who did not know enough to avoid humans. The mother, being more experienced, had streaked away in the first instant. She may still be in the area, waiting for us to leave. Or maybe she has taken advantage of the disturbance to head off for several days of hunting. When she makes a kill, she will come back and collect her kittens.

I cannot believe my good luck. Nobody gets to see a wild mountain lion. Even researchers like Martin are limited to an occasional fleeting glance. And to see one in this familiar landscape, so close to a paved road. How many times have I walked or driven past a mountain lion and never realized it?

Apparently I am not alone in my ignorance. When Martin tells people about his research, they usually look askance. "You mean there are still mountain lions out there?" they ask. "Then they must be endangered." But whether we notice them or not, the cats are definitely there—some twenty thousand in North America. Still the most widely distributed land mammal in the Western Hemisphere (apart from ourselves), mountain lions range across western Canada and the western United States, through foothills, mountains, and canyon country; rainforest, mixed woods, and chaparral. They even lick out into the prairies, by following treed river valleys into deepest Saskatchewan, Manitoba, and the Dakotas. In many western states, where grizzlies and wolves have long since been driven into extinction, mountain lions survive as the only large predators.

From the U.S.–Mexico border south, the cats make their homes in mountains, forests, grasslands, and swamps all the way to land's end in Patagonia. Nobody has a clue how many mountain lions exist in Central and South America, nor how they are coping with the human assault on tropical ecosystems.

THE LORD OF STEALTHY MURDER

Despite these large unknowns, it is fair to state that mountain lions are not endangered, taken as a whole. In other words, they are not on their deathbed as a species. At the same time, they are clearly neither as numerous nor as widespread as they were quite recently. Within the past 150 years, North American

lions (which are now confined to the western third of the continent) ranged eastward to the Atlantic coast. According to one
early writer, a Colonel H.W. Shoemaker, "The woods [of Penn-
sylvania] teemed with them.... Almost every backwoods
kitchen had a Panther [mountain lion] coverlet on the lounge
by the stove. Panther tracks could be seen crossing and re-cross-
ing all the fields, yet children on their way to school were never
molested."

Although the colonel had many seconders among frontier-
folk for his report of the "panther's" abundance, he was not
typical in his assessment of its nature. Around 1700, an Eng-
lishman named John Lawson opined (on what basis we do not
know) that "this beast is the greatest Enemy of the Planter, of
any Vermine in Carolina." Other Carolinians fed their taste for
horror by recounting tales of yowling male panthers that
preyed on pregnant women. Far and wide, the lion was feared as
a man-killer and reviled for stealing game and livestock from
innocent settlers. Even sometime-conservationist Theodore
Roosevelt blasted "the big horse-killing cat, the destroyer of
the deer, the lord of stealthy murder . . . [that faces] his doom
with a heart both craven and cruel."

Judging from present-day experience, these statements
were and are grotesque misrepresentations. True, mountain
lions do occasionally attack people, particularly small children,
but these calamities tend to be localized (Vancouver Island and
some parts of California are current hot spots) and are also rare.
On average, three or four people are killed by mountain lions
each year, making it many times more likely that you will be
killed by lightning than by a mountain lion. And though it is
true that mountain lions can learn to kill cattle and other livestock, few of them actually do. An individual sheep-eating lion

can cause big problems for a small rancher (problems the cat will likely pay for with its life), but a typical population of wild cats will never pose a significant threat to the livestock industry. As to the complaint that mountain lions steal food from the mouths of human hunters, it is hard to take such statements seriously, given the balance of power that now exists between the two species.

Belief justifies action, and the belief in a demonic, despicable panther justified an all-out assault on it. Colonel Shoemaker recounts with grief the exploits of a Black Jack Schwartz who, in 1760, rallied his friends and neighbors in Snyder County, Pennsylvania, to hold a ring hunt, or animal drive. Killed within a twenty-five-kilometer (fifteen-mile) radius were "41 Panthers, 109 Wolves, 112 Foxes, 114 Mountain Cats, 17 Black Bears, 1 White Bear, 2 Elk, 98 Deer, 111 Buffaloes, 3 Fishers, 1 Otter, 12 Gluttons [Wolverines], 3 Beavers, and upwards of 500 smaller animals."

Pennsylvania's final ring hunt was held in 1849. In the meantime, "panthers," "pumas," "cougars," "mountain cats," and "lions" had been put under bounty in that state and across the continent. California went so far as to employ professional lion hunters, with the result that an estimated 12,500 mountain lions were killed within its boundaries between 1907 and 1963. Apparently the work paid off in personal satisfaction as well as in cash. "Anybody can kill a deer," observed Ben Lilly, one of California's salaried hunters. "It takes a man to kill a varmint." The manly toil of extermination persisted until 1970, when the last of the bounties was finally cancelled.

Add to this assault the clearing of the eastern forests to create farmland, and the fate of the mountain lion was decided in eastern North America. In subsequent years, many of the hard-won farms have been abandoned and reclaimed by the forest, but though the trees have returned and the deer have returned, the mountain lions have not.

SURVIVORS

Or—just maybe—a very few have. Maybe they weren't completely wiped out after all. In 1938, several decades after the eastern population was thought to be extinct, a mountain lion was killed in northern Maine, its body stuffed and taken to the University of New Brunswick in Fredericton. This aging artifact is the last concrete proof that *Felis concolor couguar,* the eastern subspecies, might have managed to hang on. Ever since, there's been a persistent buzz of reports that the cats are still with us. Every year dozens of hunters, wildlife officers, and others come out of the forests of Ontario, Michigan, Atlantic Canada, New England, Pennsylvania, the Virginias, the Carolinas, and Georgia to certify, in tones of bug-eyed amazement, that they have seen mountain lions. Most such reports are mistaken—like the man who killed a black panther that turned out to be a house cat—but some come from qualified people and are probably accurate.

Unfortunately, a file of "probably accurate" reports does not constitute proof. And all recent attempts to produce verification, including a five-year-long study in the southern Appalachians, have come up empty-handed. Does this mean that the cats are not there or simply that they have avoided detection? Is the eastern subspecies still around? To date, the answer is a firm, well-researched "perhaps."

The only population of mountain lions that *is* known to survive east of the Mississippi is the Florida panther, *Felis concolor coryi.* Since its existence was demonstrated in 1973—there's

nothing like a live-caught cat to set the doubts to rest—
Florida's panther population has been estimated at between
thirty and fifty animals. In the opinion of experts with the
state's game commission, they exhibit "symptoms of a slow
and rather certain extinction process." Specifically, many of
them suffer from poor nutrition, because their habitat is declining in both area and quality. The cats also show signs of severe inbreeding, caused by their low numbers and by the
intrusions of industrial society, which divide the population
into ever-smaller, disconnected fragments. Several of the iden-
tifying characteristics of the Florida subspecies, such as a sharp
crook at the end of the tail, have recently been diagnosed as genetic defects. Parasites and serious diseases are widespread; the
number of kittens that survive in some areas is extremely low;
and almost all the sperm produced by the males are abnormal.

The good people of Florida have answered the call. Studies
have been funded. Nature preserves and wildlife refuges have
been enlarged. Deer hunting has been restricted. Speed limits
have been posted in critical areas to reduce roadkills. Millions
of dollars have been spent on thirty-six wildlife underpasses to
provide safe crossings of Alligator Alley, the four-lane inter-
state that rips through Fakahatchee Strand.

And even bigger challenges lie just ahead. One is to protect
panther habitat on privately owned lands, an undertaking that
could gobble up billions of taxpayers' dollars in compensation
payments. The other is to roughly triple the number of panthers by breeding them in captivity. This will involve catching
kittens (about half of which die in the wild), shipping them to
zoos and other facilities (where more of them will survive),
breeding them by artificial insemination, and shipping their
offspring back to south Florida's swampy countryside. Unless

this complex intervention succeeds, computer projections predict that the Florida panther—despite everything else that has been accomplished on its behalf—will soon be extinct.

Once an animal becomes endangered, it may be lucky enough to get intensive care, with round-the-clock, high-tech surveillance and a huge expenditure of cash and effort. Even so, it clings to life by a thread. As Charles Darwin once put it, "Rarity is the precursor to extinction," and often there is not much we can do to slow or stop the process. But what we can do, with only a moderate outlay and almost certain success, is protect healthy populations where the animals are still normally abundant and vigorous. In the case of the mountain lion, good health now lies out west.

PROTECTING ABUNDANCE

By current standards at least, western populations are flourishing. In the past twenty-odd years, they may have increased about four-fold, thanks to the elimination of bounties and removal of the species from the "varmint" category. In most western jurisdictions, mountain lions are now listed as "game animals," a classification that, with variably sized loopholes for predator "control," permits the number of killings to be limited through a licensing system. The desk work has been well done.

But the grunt work—getting out into mountain-lion country, tracking down the cats, counting their kittens to study their rate of reproduction, walking in on kills to learn about their diet, trying by fair means or foul to estimate the local population, establishing "safe" levels of hunting, studying the effects of various methods of logging, and doing it over and over, year after year, in different localities—has not received the same public endorsement. As a result, there are still many populations about which we are ignorant. "The attitude seems to be, if it's not broken, don't fix it," says wild-cat expert Maurice Hornocker who, in the late 1960s, became one of the first people to radio-collar and study wild mountain lions. "Because of tight-fisted funding, unless animals are in trouble, they don't get any attention."

The Sheep River study is one of a handful that are currently underway in Canada and the United States. Although it receives logistical support from government (for example, the use of a house and assorted "trikes" and "quads" for traveling back-country trails), it relies for money on a precarious alliance of private sponsors. In the final analysis, what keeps it going is the bone-deep dedication of Martin Jalkotzy and his two partners, Ian Ross and Ralph Schmidt. No day is too long, no hillside too steep, no trail too footsore. They carry on carrying on, unstoppable as androids.

The morning after the encounter with Geisha and her kittens, Ian is up, dressed, fed, loaded with equipment, and on the trail by 7:05. The rest of us, including two hounds named Buford and Zed, are not far behind. We spend the morning laboring through the chop of hills, sweating up steep cutlines, pausing on each likely ridge to check for guiding beeps, then plunging headlong into the next valley. Upslope and down, Buford and Zed strain at the ends of their leashes. When the cutlines end, we scramble through underbrush, over fallen logs, sliding in fresh snow. On the ascents my thighs are leaden; on the descents my kneecaps burn. Always ahead, at the edge of my field of vision, the researchers press on.

The object of their quest is a male mountain lion dubbed Thor, whose radio collar is overdue for replacement. He had not been heard from for several weeks—had the batteries that powered his transmitter already gone dead?—but yesterday he was back again, loud and clear on the radio dial. It seems he had been off exploring the frontiers of his large home range— some 300 square kilometers (115 square miles)—until urgent business called him back into radio contact. That urgent business was a female cat named Quick. Over the past several weeks, the researchers had noticed that Quick was no longer traveling with her two year-old kittens, a probable sign that she was ready to breed. Thor's timely reappearance turned that conjecture into a certainty, especially when their tracks were seen together, his as broad as an adult's hand, hers looking kittenish by comparison. Now their signals are coming from the same valley, somewhere ahead.

At the top of a small mountain, I pause to catch my breath. Behind me, in the distance, the landscape folds up on itself in misty innocence. Below, I can hear Buford and Zed baying on fresh scent, a sound that prickles the back of my neck. I head toward it.

By the time I get there, the chase is over. The howling dogs are tied around the margins of a small clearing, facing a grove of large pines, and on a broad branch overhead lies Thor, treed by some ancestral fear of baying predators. With the hullabaloo safely below him, he seems to be calm and relaxed. A heavily muscled forelimb dangles down from the branch. He looks like a burly tomcat sprawled on a giant chairback. His gaze, when he turns toward me, is piercingly direct.

From then on it is clockwork: a tranquilizing dart slaps into his hip, his body goes limp, and he is dangled with ropes to the ground. The researchers stretch him out carefully and bend over him, changing his collar, checking his teeth and claws, taking measurements. On the ground he looks small; the scale shows his weight as 60 kilograms (about 130 pounds). Not much for an animal that makes his living by killing, unaided, moose calves that are more than three times his size.

When the researchers have finished their tasks, we stand back and wait for Thor to come around. For a time the only motion is the gentle in-and-out of his breath. Then he lifts his head languorously, lets it drop, lifts it again, struggles to his feet, and stumbles off into the forest.

I think of Quick, who is out there, too, and of the two youngsters who are beginning to take up the challenges of adult life. And, of course, I remember the other young cat, the one with the searching eyes. Wordlessly, I wish them good luck and turn my thoughts toward home.

The Alberta Cougar Project came to an end two years after this account was written. With a span of a dozen years, from 1982 to 1994, it is still one of the longest and most intensive studies of mountain lions ever conducted. Tragically, researcher Ian Ross was killed in a plane crash in Kenya in 2003 while radio-tracking lions for the Laikipia Predator Project.

THE SINGING

FOREST

Diary of a Wilderness Canoe Trip

*A*UGUST 1, 2003
*From the dark wall of forest on
the opposite shore, a clear flutelike voice pours out, wistful and melan-
choly.* Dear-sweet-Can-a-da . . . dear-sweet-Can-a-da, Can-a-da,
Can-a-da. *The anthem of the boreal forest.*

It's the first morning of a six-day canoe trip, and our paddles have
brought us here, to the shore of Wallace Island at the northeast end of
Besnard Lake in central Saskatchewan. The sky glows softly with the
silver light of dawn, and at my feet, silver water ripples against ancient rocks.

Anne Janssen, one of nine fellow pavement-pounders-turned-
wannabe-voyageurs, pads up beside me, her face still soft with sleep.
"It's a white-throated sparrow," she says happily. The bird is hidden
somewhere in the foliage, and when the notes ring out again, it's as if
the song has risen from the very heart of the forest.

On the tongue of rock behind us, the rest of our party are rubbing
tired muscles and packing up their gear, preparing for a day of hard

paddling down Besnard Creek and into the Churchill River. There is no sign that anyone else has heard.

If the boreal forest is singing to us—a song of abundance, beauty, and hope—what will it take to make us stop and listen?

CANADIANS ARE A HARDY northern people who by and large prefer to live as far south as we can get. Yet even though relatively few of us actually live up north, the boreal forest—that seemingly endless scramble of rock, water, and scraggy spruce—remains the bedrock of our national experience. Extending in a broad arc from Labrador to Lake Superior and from James Bay across the northern prairie provinces to the Mackenzie Valley and southwestern Yukon, this brooding, frost-bitten landscape encompasses part of every province and territory, excluding only the Maritimes. At 5.2 million square kilometers (2 million square miles), it covers 53 percent of the country or, to put it in global terms, an area five times the size of all the countries in western Europe.

This is the iconic Canadian landscape, the inspiration of artist Tom Thomson, the natural habitat of former prime minister Pierre Trudeau. From the outset of our national adventure, it has also served us well as the powerhouse of economic development. To the extent that our economy is based on the extraction of natural resources—first furs, then minerals, oil and gas, hydro power, lumber and pulp—the great north woods have been the source of much of our wealth. If the boreal forest can be said to be etched on our collective psyche, it is also the mark of our material success, a fact that is stamped on every loonie that jingles in our pockets.

Now comes word that this "Great Green North" is more important than we ever knew, and not just to Canadians either.

According to an analysis done by the World Resources Institute in the late 1990s, Canada's boreal is one of only three large, more-or-less intact, natural forests that remain in the world, the others being the taiga, or boreal forest, of Russia and the North Amazon rain forests of Brazil. Although the southern fringe of the Canadian boreal has been scarred by development, the region is so vast and remote (not to mention buggy and cold) that much of it has been spared the effects of intensive human use. The result is a forest ecosystem that not only retains all of its life-sustaining functions—its ability to filter and purify water being high on the list—but that also provides safe haven for its full, natural complement of plants and animals. In a world where species are now blinking out at the rate of three every hour, the survival of a healthy and vibrant ecosystem, lively and complete, is an almost miraculous rarity.

Getting this message out was the purpose of the Boreal Rendezvous, a canoe-and-camping extravaganza that sent ten teams of cheerful paddlers out across the land to tackle ten of the country's great wilderness waters. Big-name rivers like the Nahanni and the Churchill were paddled by a brigade of big-name Canadians that included comedian Cathy Jones, scientist David Suzuki, and hockey great Ken Dryden, together with a variety of lesser lights. That was how I happened to find myself on the shore of Wallace Island that morning, a proud-if-paddle-weary member of Team Churchill, in the company of such luminaries as novelist Thomas King, artist Brian Deines, and Anne Janssen of the Canadian Parks and Wilderness Society, who sparked and oversaw the entire undertaking.

And it isn't just Canadians who are beating the boreal drum. Conservation of Canada's boreal forest is also the driving passion of the new kid on the block, the Canadian Boreal Initiative. Formed in 2003, CBI is a project of the Pew Charitable Trusts, a riotously wealthy family foundation based in Philadelphia. In addition to providing major funding for the Rendezvous, CBI (in conjunction with the Boreal Songbird Initiative of Seattle, another Pew storefront) has also invested in research that is designed to help us sense the color and dazzle and life of this shadowy forest. Who knew, before they told us, that all that scrubby brush was really one big aviary that produced not millions, but billions, of birds every year? Listen up, Canada; listen up, world: the boreal forest is brimming with birds.

AUGUST 2, 2003

We have two guides to lead us down the Churchill: Laurel Archer, the person who literally wrote the book on canoe travel in this neck of the woods, and Philip Roberts, a seventeen-year-old high school student from a Cree reserve called Grandmother's Bay, who has been tooling around these waters since he was a kid. When I ask Roberts how he got hired on as a guide, still so young, he says it was because he could be relied on "not to do anything stupid." But his qualifications run deeper than mere common sense. He's strong, he can read the river, and he's a good hand in a canoe. He's also a keen observer: yesterday, he picked out the faint ochre lines of a rock painting on the shore of Besnard Lake that none of us (not even Laurel) had known was there.

This morning, when we were paddling through the maze of islands and channels that is Black Bear Island Lake, somebody called out to ask him to identify a flock of birds. He checked with his binoculars and said they were coots. But after we camp, I find him sitting on a rock, studying a guidebook to Saskatchewan birds that he has borrowed from one of the other paddlers. "They weren't coots; they were this one," he says, pointing to a grebe. "So many different kinds."

THE RESEARCH COMMISSIONED by the hands-across-the-border team of Boreal Initiatives was published in May 2003 in a report entitled "The Importance of Canada's Boreal Forest to Landbirds." (Landbirds, as distinct from water birds and shore-birds, is a catch-all grouping that includes hawks, owls, wood-peckers, and songbirds, among others.) Authored by Peter Blancher—a former chief of the migratory bird populations di-vision of the Canadian Wildlife Service, now on secondment to Bird Studies Canada—the research comes with impeccable cre-dentials. Although the data on birds in the boreal region are sketchy and rely heavily on surveys in the southernmost forest fringe, Blancher has made the best of the available information and is satisfied with the overall accuracy of his conclusions. For the most part, he says, his figures are "robust" and reliable.

In a nutshell, Blancher's analysis shows that the boreal for-est is a treasure house of birds, an assertion he supports with a flight of numbers. For instance, when he tallied up the land-birds that breed in the boreal forest, the list included no fewer than 9 species of woodpeckers, 10 different finches, 11 black-birds, 15 flycatchers, 26 sparrows, 27 wood warblers, and so on, for a grand total of 186 species in 35 families. And these are just the regular breeders; another 41 species show up now and then, bringing the number to 227—almost 80 percent of the landbird species that occur in Canada.

It's not just that there are a lot of different kinds of birds flitting around in the bush. Many of the species are also ex-tremely abundant. For example, Blancher puts the boreal-breeding population of red-eyed vireos at around 70 million, and it isn't anywhere near the top of the roster. The dark-eyed junco, a natty little slate-backed sparrow that shows up at southern feeders in winter, might be the most populous species of all, with a count that may exceed 200 million. Taken to-gether, Blancher estimates that somewhere between 1 billion and 3 billion landbirds nest in the boreal each spring. By fall, when their offspring have fledged and joined them on the wing, the number surges as high as 5 billion. This amounts to 60 percent of all the landbirds in Canada and 30 percent of the population of North America. And when you think of the swimming and wading birds that rely on boreal lakes and bogs—all those coots, grebes, ducks, geese, loons, cranes, in their thousands and millions—it becomes clear that the im-portance of the region to birds cannot be overstated.

For certain species in particular, the northern forest is all there is. These are birds like the palm, Tennessee, and Con-necticut warblers, which, despite the southern affinities of their names, nest almost exclusively in the Canadian boreal forest. In fact, more than 90 percent of the global population of these three species breed in our north woods, a distinction they share with the northern shrike and the black-backed woodpecker. According to Blancher's calculations, there are another forty species, mostly flashy little warblers and sparrows, that rely on Canada's boreal forest to support at least 50 percent of their worldwide breeding population. The white-throated sparrow makes the list at 85 percent.

But what on earth are they doing here? This is the boreal forest we're talking about, not the Amazon. Isn't life supposed to falter and thin as you travel north? By rights, the boreal forest should support few species at low populations, and yet instead we find this stunning diversity and an abundance of birds. What is it about this forest that makes it so productive? And why, given its importance, is this the first we have heard about it?

AUGUST 3, 2003

Today, we take a long detour up the river to a place called High Rock Narrows. (At 48 strokes a minute for four hours, it takes 11,520 strokes to get there, but who's counting?) As the name suggests, the narrows are a tight, steep-walled channel, almost a gorge, between two islands of rock. Huge cubes of granite are piled heavily one on top of the other to form the faces of the cliffs, like blocks thrown down haphazardly from some gigantic fist. One member of our party, a Cree educator, confides that he had seen this place in a dream once, though he had never been here before. He says it is "big medicine." I didn't know that people actually used that phrase, but I know what he means.

On the flat surfaces of the granite, some unknown hand in an unknown time has inscribed images; they show strange, magical creatures and people brandishing rattles and sprouting horns. And there are pictures of birds too, wonderful birds with long, serpentine wings that scroll down like banners, framing a human figure. Birds of power and mystery.

FIONA SCHMIEGELOW is an assistant professor of Renewable Resources at the University of Alberta, a member of the Sustainable Forestry Management Network, scientific advisor to the Canadian Boreal Initiative, and a passionate advocate for sustainable use and conservation of the boreal forest. She lives, breathes, and sleeps boreal issues. But she remembers the time a few years ago when she decided to set aside her ambition of working in the cathedral forests of British Columbia and refocus her sights farther north. "I expected the boreal forest to be sort of boring compared to some of the other forests I had worked on," she says, as though startled by the thought. "Like other people, I had to learn to appreciate it. Knowing what I do now, though, I think the boreal forest is pretty magical."

As Schmiegelow sees it, Canadians have tended to take the boreal forest for granted, as a familiar but distant backdrop to everyday life. And this attitude of benign neglect has extended to scientists, with the result that worryingly little research has been conducted in boreal ecosystems. "In many cases," Schmiegelow laments, "we don't even know the specific nesting requirements of quite common boreal species." So it's little wonder that we, John and Jane Q. Public, don't know much about northern birds, if the experts haven't been paying attention to them either. Yet whatever the gaps in the current knowledge, one fact is perfectly clear. The main attraction of the boreal for landbirds is the superabundance of food.

Key, as Schmiegelow gleefully puts it, are "all those lovely mosquitoes and blackflies and horseflies, those biting insects that we love to hate, along with a whole host of other invertebrates." The bite-sized morsels provide a feeding bonanza for breeding birds and their nestlings. Because the growing season in the North is so short, the crop of invertebrates tends to come on all at once, providing an almost limitless supply of nourishment when it is needed most. Then, when winter clamps down on the forest, the birds can take to the wing and escape to the southern states, Mexico, the Caribbean, and other sun-filled getaways. Unlike most other ecosystems, in which a majority of the breeding birds are year-round residents, the birds of the boreal are mainly migrants. In fact, fully 93 percent of the landbirds in the boreal are fair-weather friends, here just long enough to catch the seasonal pulse of nutrients.

If bugs are the big attraction, they are not the whole story, Schmiegelow says. The forest's other great strength is what she calls its "intactness." It's the tree-after-tree-after-treeness of the forest—its vastness and connectivity—that allows it to meet the requirements of 186 different species. If a breeding pair cannot find what they require in one place, they can fly across the lake or to the next range of hills, until they locate the resources that will make life comfortable. For instance, Cape May and bay-breasted warblers are two of a number of species that are adapted to live in the crowns of large, old spruce, particularly those that have reached an age of 80 to 120 years. Everything about these birds equips them for life at the top. The males are bright and flashy, so they can display themselves on high branches as they stake out their territories, and their lisping, high-pitched songs carry clearly up there in sky country. What's more, their staple foods are insects such as spruce budworm and tent caterpillars that erupt in the upper branches and work their way down the tree—provided they aren't caught in the act and fed to some hungry nestling.

But the forest is not static. Old trees die of disease and blow over; they are consumed by fire. And although the forest grows back in to replace them, nothing's the same as it was before. Instead of the prickly darkness of a white spruce wood, the new forest is leafy and lush, dominated by deciduous growth, with a dense understory of shrubs and saplings. This so-called early successional forest provides ideal habitat for many species—including white-throated sparrows, American redstarts, and yellow warblers—but it has nothing to offer birds that require old-growth conifers. So the Cape May and bay-breasted warblers have to go looking for patches of forest that have made the transition from the early successional stage to mature coniferous stands.

It's the supreme mobility of birds—the enviable lightness of flight—that enables them to track the shifting resources of the forest. And this rule holds not only for old-growth species but for all kinds of boreal birds, whether they are woodpeckers searching for recently burned-over forest, chickadees looking for nest holes, or crossbills hunting for seed-laden spruce cones. "It takes very large areas of forest to maintain resources to support all those species, both in space and over time," Schmiegelow says. The miracle is that, even today, those large areas of forest are still out there.

SEPTEMBER 4, 2003

Well, we did it. In six and a half days, we paddled the entire 130-kilometer (80-mile) route from Besnard Lake to our pullout at Otter Rapids and lived to tell the tale. I am so proud of my river muscles that when I get home, I challenge my daughter to an arm-wrestling competition—and almost win.

Now, a month later, I am sitting in the belly of one of Air Canada's big birds, on my way from Saskatoon to Ottawa for the windup celebration of the Boreal Rendezvous at the Canadian Museum of Civilization. Hurtling through a cloudless sky somewhere between Winnipeg and Thunder Bay, I gaze down at the drab, green fabric of the boreal forest. It looks like an immense scratchboard painting, in shades of olive, ochre, and mauve, that blurs into the haze of cloud at the horizon. But what strikes me is not just the run of this glowering country: it is the scrawl of roads, like tangled skeins of string, that threads between reddish clearings. In a landscape that insists on the endless intricacies of its rocks and shorelines, the straight-line geometry of these clear-cuts stands out like a sore thumb. What is all this talk of an "intact" forest?

OF ALL THE INDUSTRIES that draw resources from the boreal region, logging leaves the heaviest imprint on the land. Although we have been extracting wood from these forests since the 1700s, intensive exploitation is a surprisingly recent development. In the western boreal, for example, the feller-bunchers have been at work for only the past fifteen to twenty years. But such muscle! Forestry is a major economic producer, bringing in more than U.S.$30 billion in export sales each year and providing employment to hundreds of thousands of Canadians, among them many northern residents.

Unhappily, these economic opportunities are being created at a cost to the boreal wilderness. An up-to-the-minute analysis from Global Forest Watch Canada, published in fall 2003, reveals that while the northern two-thirds of the boreal still meet the definition of intactness, the southern portion has already been seriously chewed up by industrial development— not only by heavy industry but also by the conversion of forest to farmland, a process that is continuing on an unexpectedly large scale. Alas, this worked-over tract of the forest is also highly productive for birds—the best of the best of the boreal. If their habitat is under assault, does that mean the forest's birds are on the decline?

In commissioning their report on landbirds, the twin Boreal Initiatives raised this issue with Peter Blancher, though in a way that prejudiced his response. Rather than requesting an assessment of the overall status of boreal birds, they asked, instead, for a list of species that appeared to be in trouble. The result was a catalogue of forty unfortunate species, from the olive-sided flycatcher (declining at an annual rate of 3.3 percent) to the rusty blackbird (down an alarming 10.7 percent). What the report failed to highlight was the similar number of boreal-breeding species that appear to be on the rise, birds like the red-breasted nuthatch, Lincoln's sparrow, and palm warbler, which available data suggest may be increasing at the rate of 1.4 percent, 2.1 percent, and 4.2 percent, respectively. By focusing only on problem cases and neglecting the dynamics of the forest ecosystem, with its natural ebb and flow, are conservationists creating a sense of panic without justification? It wouldn't be the first time activists have overstated their case.

Blancher is quick to acknowledge the limitations of his "trend analysis" and admits that there is no convincing evidence for any kind of general crisis. But there are no grounds for complacency, he insists, because researchers really do not know what is happening out there. Although they can say which birds are present and broadly in what abundance, they don't have enough data to track their fortunes. Ecologist Keith Hobson, a research scientist at the Prairie and Northern Wildlife Research Centre of the Canadian Wildlife Service in Saskatoon, Saskatchewan, shares this opinion. "The point is not that particular species of boreal birds are increasing, staying the same, or declining," says Hobson. "The point is that we don't *know* what is happening to them."

Whatever the present status of birds in the boreal forest, Hobson sees trouble ahead. Over the past several years, he says, 97 percent of all the merchantable timberlands in the boreal forest—the so-called working forest—has been licensed for cutting, and the shadow of industrial society is gradually creeping northward. Eventually, every scrap of salable wood in the great north woods is slated to be cut. This in itself is not a disaster. To the extent that logging is able to mimic the natural-disturbance regime of the forest—in particular, the sweep of fire—it could conceivably maintain a more or less natural flow of habitat and a full abundance of life.

Is this what we are doing now? Far from it, Hobson says. Cut blocks are too small and uniform, there are far too many roads, and the forest is being cut over too often, so that it never has a chance to attain mature old growth. "If you have less old-growth forest," he says, "you'll have fewer old-growth birds. It's not rocket science."

Things could be different. Sustainable logging, Hobson contends, "is imminently doable. The nice thing about forestry is that you can say 'By the year 2050, we want this amount of old growth on our landscape. We want this amount of burn and this amount of early successional woods.' So the GIS [geographic information system] boys get together and plug in all the data, and boom, up comes the picture and a plan. My feeling is that we can log the boreal forest sustainably for all kinds of products and still keep a lot of species happy. Call me naive, but I think it is possible."

Remarkably, here is something on which everyone seems to agree: Hobson, Schmiegelow, Blancher, and the conservation lobby. It is not too late to do things differently. Ten or twenty years from now, the time may have passed, but right now, we still have options.

"The boreal forest is mostly crown land," Schmiegelow points out. "It belongs to all of us. The question is, Do we want there to be bird song in our forest a hundred years from now?"

PEREGRINE
FALCONS

Poisoned Prospects

A pair of peregrine falcons is somewhere nearby, probably just across the river on the roof of the Bessborough Hotel in downtown Saskatoon, Saskatchewan. Eagerly, I scan the building's craggy, fairy-tale turrets, which spike above the shadows into the high dawn light. No sign of my birds.

It is early and the air is bright, one of those crystal mornings when it seems that the flick of a finger might make the whole sky ring. Below me, over the water, there is a sudden whir of flight as a flock of ducks hurtles upstream. A little distance behind them, a pair of blatting, snake-necked geese sweeps smoothly past. White gulls, their bodies held aloft on supple wings, dance in the morning light.

I settle myself on the cool grass; it could be a long wait. Peregrines are not easy to see, a Cree elder named Stan Cuthand has warned me. "It's part of what makes them special. Peregrines are mystic birds."

My binoculars swing back to the rooftop and up the tallest spire. "They go to the heights," Cuthand had said, so high that people used to think they nested on the clouds. And the way they can shoot down out of nowhere to catch other birds in the air—just fold back their wings and plummet headfirst—is a wonder. "Fantastic birds," he called them. You can never tell quite when or where they will appear.

Peregrines have been living here, on the bank of the South Saskatchewan River, for the last two summers. They now nest right in the heart of the city of Saskatoon, where they lay their eggs on window ledges and hunt pigeons from the rooftops of the high-rise towers. This is my first season close to a peregrine nest. Finally, after hours of reading and talking about them, I will have a chance to watch them fly. People say they are the fastest birds in the world—the cheetahs of the sky. Perhaps I'll be able to see for myself why they, like few other creatures, seem always to have exercised a special power over the human mind.

My fingers are already chilled and stiff on the focusing knob. Have the falcons flown off to hunt, or are they just hidden from sight? Maybe they're perched under a ledge or behind a gargoyle; maybe, right now, they're glaring down at me with their eight-power eyes. What do they make of me, staring back with my eight-power binoculars? What, for that matter, do they make of the whole urban scene that spreads out around them?

The Saskatoon falcons are one of only about fifteen thousand breeding pairs in the world, a total that puts the peregrine among the rarest of birds. It is also one of the most widely distributed species on Earth, with nests on the sea crags and cliffsides of six continents. Our pair numbers among the small but growing group of pioneers that nest in urban sites—on cathedrals and castles in Germany; on skyscrapers in Los Angeles, New York, Calgary, Montreal, and two dozen other cities in North America. Like most of these city-dwellers, the pair in Saskatoon became established with the help of humankind, as part of a worldwide effort that began in the early 1970s, when the peregrine seemed doomed to extinction from the effects of pesticides.

In an attempt to augment the failing population, biologists in several countries bred falcons in captivity and released them into the wild. Saskatoon's male was hatched at the local university and turned loose from the roof of the Bessborough. The next spring, he made headlines in the local press by coming back to claim a territory. But scientists can't take credit for finding him a mate—she arrived of her own accord. She likely came from somewhere in the northern wilderness, but no one is sure. Nor can anyone explain why she showed up at just the right time to join the captive-reared male. How did she know the male was here, and why did she choose to settle above the asphalt and neon lights?

I pull my coat closer around me and study the skyline again, this time panning slowly to the south. A squat form perched on the corner of an office tower takes off in a haze of motion, then soars on backswept wings. Watch out, pigeon. Those falcons would love to capture you.

But what is this? On the roof of the neighboring tower, twenty-five stories high, there is a tall antenna and, on top of that, spotlit by the sun, sits a bird. I focus frantically. Yes, dark head, light bib and chest, sleek contours, a little larger than a crow. Lazily, the bird stretches out one very long, sharp-pointed wing, slightly crooked at the "wrist." It must be a peregrine.

So let the show begin! Fly for me, since that's your specialty. I remember the spectacular courtship displays I have read about, especially a report by Joseph A. Hagar that I'd found in an old bird book, *Life Histories of North American Birds of Prey:*

> Again and again the [male Peregrine]... started well to leeward and came along the cliff against the wind, diving, plunging, saw-toothing, rolling over and over, darting hither and yon like an autumn leaf until finally he would swoop up into the full current of air and be borne off on the gale to do it all over again. At length he tired of this, and, soaring in narrow circles without any movement of his wings other than a constant small adjustment of their planes, he rose to a position 500 or 600 feet above the mountain and north of the cliff. Nosing over suddenly, he flicked his wings rapidly 15 or 20 times and fell like a thunderbolt. Wings half closed now, he shot down past the north end of the cliff, described three successive vertical loop-the-loops across its face, turning completely upside down at the top of each loop, and roared out over our heads with the wind rushing through his wings like ripping canvas.... The sheer excitement of watching such a performance was tremendous; we felt a strong impulse to stand and cheer.

How I'd love to see something like that! But the sun-warmed falcon on the rooftop doesn't want my applause. After a few minutes, it launches itself easily into the sky and soars in an unhurried arc around the building. Then, cutting the air briskly with strong, quick strokes, it heads upstream. I squint through the binoculars, straining to follow, but within seconds the bird is a speck and the speck is lost from sight.

So that's that: I have seen a peregrine. For this I have crawled out of bed at the crack of dawn and waxed poetic in the cold and damp? For this hundreds of people have filled thousands of pages with observations and data? This is the bird that has inspired a multimillion-dollar recovery program? What is all the fuss about?

Yet quick on the heels of disappointment comes a rush of delight. As I walk home through the quiet streets, I realize that something has changed in me, not so much through glimpsing the peregrine as through the simple act of watching for it. It is as if I, and not just the morning, have now been filled with fresh clear light. To be out-of-doors at sunrise with every sense alert, attuned to the slightest movement, to the cut of every wing. To hear the bird song from the bushes, the woodpecker drumming on a nearby stump—that in itself has been worth something. It has shaken me out of the numbness of my everyday consciousness.

Sitting and waiting, with the river at my feet, I have known what it means to be alive and part of a living world. Is this what peregrine watchers have always been shown? I suddenly think of something else that Stan Cuthand said. Peregrines are messengers, he told me. They bring guidance from the Great Spirit, which was here before the world began and reveals itself to people through the creatures of this world. "Peregrines are mystic birds." Was this what he had meant?

GETTING THE MESSAGE

Across the river, on the very rooftop where I had seen my first peregrine, a gate opens and a man lets himself over the wall. He dangles across a steep glass face and scrambles into a window well outside the twenty-fourth floor. Only a knee-high railing screens the drop to the street.

Above the climber, peering over the edge, are more men, some with TV cameras poised to record his descent. And above them, in the air, hang two peregrines, the sturdy, wide-winged female and her more delicate mate. At first both falcons seem relaxed, wheeling in large, easy loops, but when the man reaches the window well, they cut in tightly over his head and start to scream.

I am at my usual post on the riverbank, peering up through binoculars, but the calls carry across the water, a shrill, irritated, furious, relentless bombardment of sound. *Ka-ka-ka-ka-kak*. And even though I can't see everything that is happening behind the rail, I know why the birds are alarmed. The man is standing in the cranny where they have scraped out a nest. At his feet sprawl three young falcon chicks, little round-eyed balls of fluff, all bellies, beaks, and claws.

Last year, when a similar scene was played out, there had only been one youngster in the falcons' nest, but when the climber left and the birds returned to their ledge, they found their family had suddenly grown to four. Though the peregrines could scarcely have understood, the three extra youngsters had been hatched in captivity, carried in by the climber, and left for the falcons to raise. At first the adult birds hung back, uncertain what to make of this daunting gift, but they soon recovered from their shock and spent the rest of the summer hunting to keep the family fed. That fall, four well-fed young falcons flew from the rooftops and headed south to their wintering grounds in Central and South America.

This year, with three chicks of their own, the adult falcons already have their work cut out for them, and the climber has not brought them any more. All he wants to do is band their babies and leave. But the falcons, aware only of the danger to their young, are now in a total uproar. They scream and circle;

they dive. First one, then the other climbs the sky and launches itself like a missile toward the window well. The intruder doubles over, his face down and his back to his birds; he looks awkwardly over his shoulder to see what is coming at him. Again and again the falcons plunge, within inches of his skin—yet somehow, at the last instant, they zip past, carve a hairpin bend, and tear up and away without touching him.

"It's pretty exciting," says Paddy Thompson, who has supervised the banding trip, when I speak to him afterward. But what he has in mind is not the rush of the falcons' aggressive flight. Instead, he is thinking of the simple fact that the pair has hatched more young this year than ever before. Three chicks is a healthy, normal brood, a number that bodes well for the future. Last year, with its single chick, and the year before, with none, had raised anxious doubts. Perhaps the male and female were not compatible, or the female was too old to produce well (no one knew her history). Or worst of all, maybe she had been poisoned by DDT and could not breed properly.

It is frustrating that even now—decades after DDT was blacklisted in Canada, the United States, and most of western Europe—there is still reason to worry about peregrines' reproductive health. Even now, peregrines from many localities carry worrisome amounts of DDT and other organochlorines in their bodies. How can this be? The answers, as usual, are complex. In some places, DDT has hung around in the environment ever since it was put there back in the 1950s and 1960s. Chemical stability was one of the characteristics that made DDT so attractive as an insect poison in the first place: it was not easily broken down by sun, wind, rain, or biological activity, and it could go on killing long after it was applied. Its half life in ocean sediments (the length of time for 50 percent of the chemical to break down) may be as long as 150 years.

And there is another source of contamination that is more troubling—the continuing use of DDT and "other compounds of extinction" in Central and South America, Africa, India, and other parts of the Third World. Even after the use of organochlorines was restricted in the First World, it remained legal for companies to manufacture the chemicals for export or to produce and sell them offshore. So when markets for DDT dried up in the wealthy countries, the manufacturers promptly offered their wonder-working pesticide—proven effective, nontoxic to humans, and, above all, cheap—to the "developing" nations, as a weapon in their struggle against hunger and disease. As a result, the use of DDT simply shifted south.

When DDT and the other organochlorines were restricted in the First World, we had a choice. We could have set to work wholeheartedly to develop alternatives to chemical pest control. We could have followed what Rachel Carson, in 1962, was already mapping out as "The Other Road." Instead, we reached onto the laboratory shelf for another kind of insect killer. For the organochlorines, a product of Allied wartime research, we substituted a group of chemicals known as carbamates and another family of compounds called organophosphates, which had been developed by the German military in their search for chemical weapons. To these insect poisons we then added a bewildering diversity of weed killers and fungicides.

The situation would be unbearable were it not for one fact. We do have alternatives; we do not have to go on clubbing the Earth with these brutal technologies. We know, from studies that have now been conducted in several parts of the world, that "organic" farms, where food is grown with little or no pesticide, support significantly more birds and more bird species than those on which pesticides are used. We know, from data collected and analyzed by the National Research Council of the

United States, that low-pesticide and no-pesticide farming can be highly productive and highly profitable. We know, from the example of Sweden, which is well on its way to a 50 percent reduction in pesticide use, that people and nations can decide to stand on the side of life.

As Rachel Carson told us in *Silent Spring,* "The choice . . . is ours to make. . . . We should no longer accept the counsel of those who tell us that we must fill our world with poisonous chemicals; we should look about and see what other course is open to us."

We know which road we must take. And that road takes us back to the peregrine falcon again, back through the lessons of the recent past and, farther still, back to the message of hope that the falcon has long been empowered to bring. "Peregrines are birds that stretch the imagination," somebody said to me, and with imagination comes hope. We are not trapped by the past. We can create the future we need, under the falcon's wing.

Since this account was written, the effort to save the peregrine in North America has paid off dramatically. By the late 1990s, the population of the anatum subspecies (the mid-continent population that was most severely affected by DDT) had rebounded from near extinction to an estimated three thousand breeding pairs. In 1999, the species was removed from the endangered list in the United States and downlisted from endangered to threatened in Canada. DDT, the chemical that caused the problem, was banned from North America and western Europe by the 1970s. Since then, however, overall pesticide use has increased dramatically. According to the U.S. Department of Agriculture, the amount of active ingredients used annually on American croplands has risen from around 300 million tonnes, or tons, in 1970 to over 500 million tonnes, or tons, in 2001. Although the peregrine has been rescued from extinction, the rain of toxins has not stopped.

A FEAST

of Facts

THE NATURE
OF WOLVES

Wild Lives

$\mathcal{T}$he itch of human curiosity being what it is, there are probably many things you want to know about wolves: how big they get, how fast they run, how many pups they have, whether it's really true that they can communicate over long distances. You may be interested in their family lives, their hunting strategies, and their importance as predators.

Surprisingly, the best place to begin this exploration is inside a wolf's mouth. Wolves have forty-two teeth, which fall into the same general categories as our own—incisors, canines, premolars, and molars. Three special features of this arsenal call for our attention: first, the sheer number of teeth. (Mountain lions, by contrast, have only thirty.) The need to make room for them all and deploy them usefully probably accounts for the wolf's long snout. Notice next the four pointed canines, or "dog teeth," near the front of the jaw on the bottom and top. As long as penknife blades, these teeth are the functional equivalent of talons and permit a wolf to pierce through tough hides and thick hair—and hang on. Thus equipped, a wolf can bite through the flesh of a woolly muskox or hook its fangs into the pendulous nose of a moose and cling fast, no matter how much the animal thrashes about.

The third feature to note is the set of massive craggy molars toward the back of the mouth. These specialized shearing teeth, known as carnassials, are one of the reasons that the modern line of carnivores has managed to survive. You could find them, if you dared, in the mouths of bears, weasels, tigers, and the two hundred other members of the order Carnivora, the evolutionary line to which wolves belong.

You could also find them, at less personal risk, in the mouth of a pet dog. In fact, you would find all forty-two wolf teeth there, in somewhat modified form. This is because wolves and dogs are close kin. Although the subject continues to be controversial, most authorities agree that all dogs, from chihuahuas to Dobermans, are descended from wolves that were tamed in the Near East ten thousand to twelve thousand years ago. Others speculate that wolves were domesticated then and at several other places and times. There is no longer any serious argument in favor of another species as a major point of origin—coyote, fox, or any other member of the wild dog family. (In North America, coyotes, wolves, and dogs all occasionally interbreed to produce coy-wolf, coy-dog, and wolf-dog hybrids, so it is likely that the dog line carries a little coyote blood.)

Why were wolves singled out for this intimate recognition as the first domesticated animal and "man's best friend"? To answer this question, we must look at the ways in which wolves differ from other members of the wild dog family. For one thing, wolves take first place for size. Although smaller in fact than in legend, adult females weigh between about 20 and 55 kilograms (45 and 120 pounds), and males may be 70 kilograms (155 pounds) or more. On average, tip to tail, they measure about one and a half meters (four to five feet) in length and stand three-quarters of a meter (thirty inches) high at the shoulder. They are, in other words, very big dogs, larger in every dimension than a standard German shepherd. By taming wolves, people allied themselves with this impressive strength and size.

Early hunting peoples also took advantage of wolves' superior speed. More than any other carnivores, these far-ranging animals are adapted to run. For one thing, they and other wild dogs enjoy the runner's leggy build. For another, canines have moved up off the flat of their feet and onto their toes for extra speed. But the specialization that sets wolves apart is the anatomy of their front legs, which are "hung" close together, almost as if pressed into the animals' narrow chests. Their knees turn in and their paws turn outward, allowing their front feet to set a path which the hind feet follow precisely. When they are trotting, wolves leave a neat, single line of tracks, an advantage for efficient travel in deep snow or on difficult terrain. Thanks to these physical refinements, wolves can run at sixty to seventy kilometers (thirty-five to forty-five miles) per hour when pressed.

FAMILY VALUES

The aspect of the wolf's nature that may have had the strongest appeal to the first would-be dog owners, as it does for us today, is the animals' affectionate interest in their families. More than any other canid, wolves are social animals. Although some individuals live singly for periods of time (the proverbial "lone wolves"), the usual context of a wolf's life is a small kinship grouping, or pack, that includes mother and father, uncles and aunts, and siblings. Pack sizes, like most other wolf traits, vary considerably, from a single pair, which is quite common, to a community of forty-two (recorded in northern Alberta), which is very rare. Most wolves live in groups of seven animals or less.

The overriding theme of wolf society is amiability. In the late 1930s, a patient biologist named Adolph Murie spent two summers observing at a wolf den in Denali (then Mount McKinley) National Park in Alaska, as part of the first-ever scientific study of wild wolves. (The results of his efforts were published in 1941 as *The Wolves of Mount McKinley*.) "The strongest impression remaining with me after watching the wolves on numerous occasions," he wrote, "was their friendliness." This was despite all the inevitable irritations of family life: a pup who wants to jump on your head, a sibling who hogs the best sleeping place, an elder who eats more than his share, and so on.

One key to the generally even-tempered atmosphere of a wolf pack is clear communication. Like people, wolves have expressive faces. Through subtle gestures of the forehead, mouth, ears, and eyes, an animal can "say" how it feels and thus permit its companions to react appropriately. For example, if a wolf is afraid or insecure, it keeps its teeth covered ("see, I would never bite you"), pulls the corners of its mouth back in a smile-like "submissive grin," narrows its eyes to slanting slits, smooths its forehead, and flattens its ears against its head. A confident, threatening expression is just the reverse: bared teeth, mouth corners forward, wrinkled muzzle, frowning forehead, and erect, forward-pointing ears.

Human expressions are amazingly similar. Try making an ingratiating face, as if you want to ease out of a confrontation with a bully; then scowl as if you are ready to bite off someone's head. Chances are you won't be able to say much with your ears, but otherwise your facial gestures will likely resemble those of a wolf in similar circumstances.

It is much easier for a human being to intuit the mood of a wolf or dog than that of a hamster, say, or a canary. As photographer Jim Brandenburg put it after a summer spent watching wolves in the High Arctic, "I've never seen animals that have so many characteristics that can be felt." No wonder early peoples chose wolves for their companions.

If the first dog was pure wolf, modern dogs are so distinct from their ancestors that they are considered by many scientists to be a separate species. *Canis lupus* has become *Canis familiaris.* In addition to the obvious differences that have been bred into certain lines, other more subtle changes have taken place. Even the most wolflike of modern dogs tend to have smaller teeth, shorter muzzles, and broader foreheads than wolves, making them look a little more like their human masters. They are also said to be less intelligent than their wild cousins, a common result of domestication. (It would be interesting to know if this rule holds for humans, as well.) Dogs breed twice a year rather than once, lack certain glands on the tail, and have distinctively shaped skulls. To human eyes, their feet seem to be "the right size," rather than "too big" like those of their snowshoed, wild relatives. But the most significant difference is in their social attitude: dogs want to be with people, wolves want to be with wolves. The bonds of affection that connect a dog to its favorite humans are probably very similar to those that form among a pack of wolves.

PEACE, ORDER, AND GOOD GOVERNMENT

Wolf packs are loosely hierarchical. A large, well-established pack may consist of a small "upper class" that includes only a single breeding pair (the so-called alpha male and female), a "middle class" of nonbreeding adults, perhaps an "underclass" of outcasts, and an up-and-coming group of pups and immature animals who are less than two years of age. The leaders of the pack, usually the parents of the younger animals, wear their status with confidence. In social encounters, they stand tall, hold their ears and tails erect, and look other animals directly in the eyes. Simply by doing this, they are declaring and reinforcing their superior rank. A subordinate animal, on the other hand, slips toward the leader on bent legs, tail low and ears slicked back. Like a pup begging for food, it bunts its nose against the superior's face in greeting, as if to say, "I'm little and you're big; I like you, so please be nice to me." This gesture has been dubbed "active submission." If the subordinate animal feels a need to make its point more emphatically—"I accept that you are the leader and that I am a social underling; I'm no threat to you"—it may sprawl on its back with its feet in the air, exactly like a dog that wants its belly scratched. This behavior, known as "passive submission," may also carry a reference to infancy, because it is very like the position of a tiny pup that is being massaged by an adult to make its bowels work. You can look for these dominance/submission routines in the wolf cage at the zoo, or see how the wolves react if you use your hands to mimic ears-up and ears-back postures. (Ironically, most of our intimate knowledge of these spirits of the wilderness has been gained by observing animals in captivity.)

With a bit of luck, you may also have a chance to watch a wolf greeting ceremony, one of those noisy, wagful, face-licking get-togethers in which the animals rediscover one another after waking from a snooze or reunite after a brief separation. In the wild, these celebrations of family solidarity also often occur before a hunt when the animals scent prey or after a kill. Frequently, the focus of the festivities is the alpha male—often the most popular animal in the pack—who suddenly finds himself closely surrounded by half a dozen eager, howling relatives, all doing their best to plaster up beside him and stick their muzzles in his face. Through this affectionate ritual, the animals define their group ("this is us; all other wolves are outsiders") and reaffirm their attachment to their father and to one another.

As a rule, a dominant male wolf is not particularly aggressive, at least toward other members of his group. In fact, the opposite is likely to be true: most top-ranking male wolves are exceptionally tolerant. Wolves in a pack are constantly checking one another, with a sniff to the coat here, a lick on the cheek there; and no animal is more active in receiving this kind of routine social contact than the dominant male. He provides an emotional center for the community and a focus for friendly feeling in the family.

MOTHERHOOD

ISSUES

Mammals and the Maternal Instinct

*T*he idea that females are endowed with an innate "maternal instinct" is a venerable one. But the fact is that mammals are not all born with an insatiable yearning to care for young. A virgin female rat, for example, typically shows every sign of detesting pups. Forced into their presence, she draws away, closes her eyes, and generally acts as if she is horrified by the mere fact of their existence. She may even try to bury them in bedding, in an attempt to keep their disagreeable odor away from her nose and whiskers. Yet when this same female becomes pregnant, she will find herself enamored of the little darlings—the very same infants whom, a week or two before, she had despised with her whole heart.

Biologist Ruth Ewer, author of *The Ethology of Mammals,* once witnessed a similar transformation in the attitude of a female house cat toward one of her weaned kittens. Pregnant with a new litter, the mother cat acted as if she had come to hate her half-grown son, whom she repelled with hissing and claws whenever he appeared. This went on for weeks. Then, just before she was ready to give birth, he happened to approach, perhaps expecting the worst, and instead found himself licked and caressed like the most lovable kitty on Earth. "In the brief space of half an hour he had metamorphosed from an undesirable, to be driven away at all costs, into an object of extreme maternal solicitude."

An animal's inclination to care for her young can be switched on and off by her hormones. In the lab, a virgin female rat with a taste for killing pups can be quickly transformed into an attentive caregiver. The simplest way is to give her injections of three chemicals: the female sex hormones estrogen and progesterone and a pregnancy hormone called prolactin. In the normal scheme of things, these substances are produced by the endocrine glands, the placenta, and the fetus itself (making a covert bid for its mother's care).

Under the influence of this elixir, a mother-to-be often begins to make preparations for the birth of her offspring by gathering nest material or starting work on her den. At the same time, she may develop a passionate interest in her neighbor's young, even to the point of baby-snatching. A pregnant mouse, for example, may grab a stray pup, hold it down with her paws, and groom it enthusiastically before letting it go. A female sheep may actually steal another ewe's lamb and forcibly keep the bleating mother at a distance. But when the kidnapper gives birth herself, her captive loses its charm, and she directs her maternal fervor toward her own newborn.

There is nothing especially tender about the act of giving birth. Yet surprisingly, the physical trauma of birthing turns out to be another important stimulus for maternal tenderness.

The muscular rending and stretching that propel infants out into the world also send powerful signals coursing through the mother's nerves. These messages trigger changes in her brain, which in turn influence her hormones—and her behavior. Thus a ewe will not normally adopt an unfamiliar youngster. But if her cervix is manipulated to simulate giving birth, she is likely to accept any lamb that is presented to her.

The physical sensations of parturition are just the first stage in the sensory extravaganza of birthing. As each infant emerges from the vagina, an animal mother is treated to an array of pleasing tastes and scents. Eagerly, she grasps the newborn with her paws, draws it toward her mouth, and begins to lick it with gusto. In the process, she not only washes off amniotic fluid and removes the birth membranes, she also stimulates the nerves that control the infant's first intake of breath. (Sometimes a mother goat becomes so intent on licking that she totally frustrates her youngster's attempts to stand or to nurse. Every time it tries to rise, she pushes it down with her foot. If, conversely, she fails to lick it at all, it is likely to lie down and die.) Finally, to complete her postpartum feast, the mother eagerly eats the afterbirth. Although her willingness to consume this mess wanes after she's given birth, virtually every mammalian mother experiences a momentary enthusiasm for eating gooey membranes—with one fortunate exception. Indeed, one wag has suggested that our species be defined "as the primate that does not normally eat the placenta."

BONDING WITH BABY

As the cumulative effect of all these experiences, the female enters what biologists call the "maternal state," which renders her willing and able to provide care for infants. In some species, this is a generalized response to any and all youngsters. A mother rat, for example, will cross an electrified grid to rescue young infants, regardless of whether they are her own or someone else's. In one experiment, a rat brought in a total of fifty-eight youngsters and would have gone after even more if the scientists hadn't run out of pups for her to carry home. In other trials, rats have been known to retrieve mice, rabbits, chicks, and even kittens in a superabundance of maternal zeal.

As far as we can tell, many species of rodents and some carnivores (including house cats) cannot recognize their own offspring. In the laboratory, these animals will care for any infant they are offered. But in nature, they seldom become confused, because their young are kept sequestered in private dens or in secluded corners of the forest. Any infant that's in the right place is likely to have the right parentage. Mammals that mix and mingle, on the other hand, generally have a better sense of who's who. A prairie gopher (or Richardson's ground squirrel) will nurse any pup that is dropped down her nest hole; but as soon as the youngsters come out to play with their age-mates in the colony, she refuses to accept any except those she has raised. Unable to identify her youngsters when it was unnecessary, she quickly learns to recognize them by scent, sight, and voice when it becomes important for her to do so.

For some species of mammals, bonding with baby—getting to know one's own offspring as an individual—matters from the moment of birth. A Mexican free-tailed bat, for example, bears her pup in a bustling nursery cave. When she goes off to feed, she leaves her infant hanging from the rocks, cheek by jowl with ten thousand other almost-identical youngsters. There seems little hope she will ever see it again, one among so many thousands. Indeed, for many years, scientists believed that returning females simply permitted themselves to be suckled by any infant that managed to grasp hold of a nipple. But DNA studies have shown that a mother bat does locate and nurse her own pup, even in this throng, on well over 80 percent of her trips home. She is assisted in this feat by a faint glandular scent with which she marks her pup and by its eager response to her homecoming vocalizations. "It's me, Mom. Over here."

Nobody knows exactly when and how bats form this attachment to their infants. Does the process take time? Does it ever fail? But we do know something about a similar process in sheep and goats. Sheep, for instance, live in tight flocks that offer plenty of scope for confusion and accidental baby-swaps. To guard against this possibility, ewes experience a period of heightened awareness in the first few hours after giving birth, during which they are exquisitely sensitive to the taste and smell of their newborns. In as little as ten minutes of licking and sniffing, a mother sheep memorizes the unique olfactory signature of her youngster. Thereafter, she will accept no other; indeed, she violently repels any pretenders. But if her lamb is taken from her at birth and kept away for a few hours, the window of sensitivity closes and she treats it like a total stranger. The moment has been lost and the lamb abandoned.

In most ways that matter, women are remarkably unlike ewes. Yet for the last twenty-five years, the mother-infant bonding of sheep has been widely accepted as an appropriate model for humans. According to scholar Diane E. Eyer, author of *Mother-Infant Bonding: A Scientific Fiction,* this "craze" was born in the 1970s, as the offspring of bad science and rapid social change. Despite its dubious parentage, the theory flourished because, on the one hand, it appealed to social conservatives, who wanted women to stay at home. At the same time, the idea met the needs of working mothers, who liked the thought that parent-child attunement could be assured by a little quality time immediately after birth. Ever since, experts have solemnly advised us that the first hours or days of life are crucially important to the mother-infant bond, as if people, like sheep, had a tightly defined sensitive period. Yet there is no evidence that this is true.

Similarly, many psychologists stress the critical importance of a secure relationship between baby and its "primary caregiver" (a.k.a. "mother"), as if human childcare were inevitably an isolated, one-on-one project—one lamb, one ewe—rather than a familial or communal undertaking. The evidence on this point is, at best, ambiguous, as competing studies conclude that multiple caregivers are, or are not, beneficial to very young children. Perhaps in the end it will turn out that humans are less like sheep and more like wolves, lions, elephants, and other social mammals, among whom infants form bonds not only with their mothers but also with their sisters, aunts, grandmothers, and, in the most companionable species, their brothers, uncles, and dads.

CLEVER

CORVIDS

A Mind for Food

*B*rainy animals tend to take a carnal delight in food—flower and fruit, fish and fowl, animal and vegetable. They are often "generalists," able to identify and exploit a wide array of nutritional resources. Whereas a specialized animal may be able to get by with low mental wattage (just enough to permit it to recognize a few preferred foods), a generalist has to run a regular inventory on dozens of edible items, an occupation that calls for curiosity, perception, memory, and, often, inventiveness. For such an animal, a well-stocked brain may be an essential means to a well-stuffed belly.

Most species of corvids (a group of birds that includes crows, ravens, magpies, and jays) have wide-ranging tastes in food. Almost all are omnivores and typically seek food both in trees and on the ground—seeds, nuts, berries, caterpillars, grasshoppers, frogs, field mice, garbage, carrion, and other delicacies. The birds appear to be born with an innate ability to recognize and acquire some of these items. Eurasian jays go through a stereo-typed (and presumably inborn) routine when they catch wasps, which involves capturing the insect and then biting repeatedly near the stinger to disable it. Jays do not have to learn the hard way to avoid this hazard. But they are nonetheless highly capable of learning about other dangers in their food supply. For example, when a captive jay was fed two species of grasshopper, one poisonous and one safe, the bird hungrily gobbled up both of them. But once was enough. Even though the insects were ingested together, the jay somehow identified the culprits and thereafter refused to eat them any more, although it continued to welcome the more palatable kind.

It seems likely that the foraging behavior of many corvids is largely shaped by experience. Their education may well begin in the nest, as they become familiar with the items their parents bring to them, and continue during the weeks when they hang around home as fledglings. Young jays, for example, are not born knowing about the relationship between small acorns and mighty oaks. When they first see oak seedlings, the birds take no interest in them. But once they notice adults obtaining nuts from beneath the plants, the youngsters begin to pull at all sorts of vegetation. In time, either through trial-and-error learning or closer observation of their parents, they learn to restrict their efforts to oaks and, even more specifically, to the first-year plants that are most likely to yield edible cotyledons.

Even as adults, corvids are constantly on the lookout for clues about what's on today's menu. To obtain up-to-the-minute information, they keep a sharp eye on other members of their flock or family group. Has one of them found a feast that could be shared? Has someone found a smaller prize that could be stolen or duplicated? Crowd around and take a look. Don't stand back; it pays to be curious. If one of your companions flies strong and hard away from the nighttime roost, follow it eagerly in the hope that it is heading for food. When a flustered songbird rages and swoops at you, take it as a sign that it has eggs or chicks nearby and calmly search the bushes. Watch the ducks come and go from the marsh until you know where to look for their nests. For an experienced corvid, the airwaves are crackling with information.

SEARCH IMAGES

No one knows how, or if, birds think about what they learn. But biologists suspect that they store their knowledge in the form of "search images." In one laboratory experiment, a group of blue jays was trained to peck a key and obtain a food reward whenever they saw a picture of a certain species of moth. At first, the moths were shown against plain cards so that their color and form could be clearly observed. But later they were pictured in their natural cryptic environment. Even though the insects now blended almost perfectly into the background, the trained jays still picked them out with little difficulty. By contrast, they seldom responded to similar images of a different type of moth, presumably because they had not formed a search image for this species and could not detect it under camouflage conditions.

The classic demonstration of search images was made in 1970 by a researcher with the fitting name of Harvey Croze. On a sandy beach where carrion crows gathered mussels, Croze laid out a row of empty shells, each with a piece of meat beside it. Within a few hours, the crows had found and eaten all these tidbits. The next day, Croze set out another row of shells, only this time he hid the food underneath them. When the crows returned, all they could see were empty shells on the sand, a sight that would not ordinarily spark their curiosity. Yet the birds found, overturned, and fed from all but two of them. From a single experience, they had learned that empty mussel shells could be a sign of food and had apparently formed a search image for them.

Once learned, never forgotten. Even when Croze began setting out shells without meat in them, the crows continued to investigate them now and then. If he baited one at random, the crow that hit the jackpot would suddenly turn its attention to checking empty shells, in a single-minded attempt to strike it lucky again.

The last phase of Croze's experiment, in which the birds were winners and losers by turns, begins to approach the complexity of real-life foraging. It's a game of chance, and the stakes are literally life and death. If you consistently score, you will obtain enough energy to survive and reproduce. But if you lose too often, you burn up more calories in the search for food than you take in from what you ingest. Even crows and ravens, birds that are reputed to "eat anything," have to be selective in their food choices. To do this, they must constantly scan their home range for possible nourishment, like the crows that kept a watchful eye on Croze's mussel shells. Then they must determine which of their options is currently the best bet. (Thus, a crow that found a baited shell immediately put its money on searching for more of them.) And finally, as the source of food on which they are foraging becomes depleted, they must decide when it's time to head for greener pastures. How much energy does it pay to expend on checking mussel shells? At what point would you be better off to search for fruit in the cherry orchard or hunt for insects in the bushes? Somehow, corvids make these choices and make them well.

OPTIMAL FORAGING

In the words of one expert, studies of foraging behavior generally imply that "animals are capable of sophisticated behavior involving subtle discriminations and decision-making." Certainly, corvids choose their food with astonishing shrewdness. Pinyon jays, for example, are able to distinguish nutritious pine seeds from worthless ones by checking them for color, weight, and the sound they make when clicked in the bill. Similarly, Eurasian jays inspect and handle acorns to determine which are large and sound enough to be worth bothering with. If the jays want to transport several nuts to a caching site, they must again rank them by size, with smaller ones being stowed down in the throat and larger ones (too wide to swallow) loaded into the beak. "During close observations" made in Holland (as reported by I. Bossema in the journal *Behaviour*), "it was sometimes seen that a jay approached a thick acorn first, made an intention movement to seize it (without touching), went to smaller ones and swallowed these. It then returned to the big one and transported it in the bill without attempting to swallow it." Jays, it seems, are always thinking.

When Reto Zach investigated the feeding behavior of crows on Mandarte Island, British Columbia, he discovered that they also evaluated food items—specifically, snails or whelks—by size. The crows chose only the heaviest prey, sometimes picking up and discarding several shells before settling on ones they liked. Larger whelks had two advantages over small ones, Zach found: they yielded more food and were easier to open. The crows cracked the shells by dropping them on the shore or, to be more precise (as the crows certainly were), on a level floor of rock on the landward side of the beach. Here the shells broke readily on the hard surface and were prevented from rolling into the water by the slope and location of the dropping site.

The crows dropped the shells from an average height of five meters (about sixteen feet)—the very height that Zach determined from his experiments to be most efficient for breaking large whelks. Had the crows flown higher to make the drop, they would have wasted energy and, at the same time, increased the chance that the shell would bounce out of sight or shatter, filling the meat with shell chips. (As it was, "several crows were seen dipping broken whelks in fresh water puddles before eating," as if to rid their meal of unpleasant grit.)

All in all, as Zach reported in *Behaviour,* the "crows achieved close to the maximum foraging efficiency possible for breaking whelks." The only way he could see for them to improve their performance was by dropping two whelks at a time. And sure enough, one of the crows achieved just that refinement. Without drawing a single bar graph, the crows did everything right.

AURORA
BOREALIS

Airy Nothings

*I*t is dark. Not the phony dark of a modern, overlit city, but true dark and cold. The yellow glow of camp fades quickly behind us, eclipsed by the forest and the dense night.

Two vague forms, our silhouettes muffled with winter clothes, we shuffle out of the spruce woods, through a thicket of willows, and onto the surface of a small lake. A little distance into this clearing, my companion stops. "Look," she says quietly, waving a mittened hand. "Look up."

Ribbons of frosty breath stream from our upturned faces. Far above, ribbons of soft greenish light stream across the sky. Aurora borealis, the northern lights.

From horizon to horizon, misty dragons swim through the heavens. Green curtains billow and swirl. Fast-moving, sky-filling tissues of gossamer. Through them in the farther distance, we can see the familiar pinpoint outlines of star patterns: Great Bear and her son, Little Bear; sinuous Draco; exact Cassiopeia; Polaris, the hub.

Apart from the hush of our breathing, nothing can be heard. We lean our heads together and speak in whispers.

We are grown women, my friend and I. Indeed, if the somber truth is to be told, we are middle-aged—well educated, well traveled, well read; and here, near the shore of Great Slave Lake in the Canadian territories, the northern lights are a privileged commonplace. We have often seen them before. Yet we stand transfixed, in the middle of the night, in the middle of a snowy pond, watching the aurora dance overhead.

By rights, we humans ought to live in constant wonderment, amazed by every star, cloud, tree, leaf, feather, fish, and rock. Amazed by the supreme improbability of our own intricate existence. But except for a gifted few (artists and mystics), we lack the stamina for so much mystery. It takes a shock—a sudden burst of beauty—to wake us to the wonder of our reality.

What power brings the sky to life with these soft, streaming curtains of light? How can they write themselves across the night and then vanish, without a trace, into the darkness? Where do they come from? Where do they go? What prompts them at one moment to hang quietly over the horizon, an unobtrusive arc of whitish light? At another, still formless and diffuse, to flutter in the zenith with a steady, flashing pulse? At yet another to unfurl themselves in rushing, swirling bands of green and pink that eddy, flow, and crack the whip in the silence?

Does all this heavenly glory have some deep meaning? What do the lights have to tell us about the mysterious stardust universe into which we are born?

Under the gaze of modern science, the polar lights have turned out to be even more wondrous than we had imagined. Seen from space, the aurora is revealed as two broken rings of light, each about 4,000 kilometers (2,500 miles) in diameter, that hover over the polar regions of the Earth. What's more, these haloes, or aural ovals, appear simultaneously and symmetrically in both the Northern and Southern Hemispheres. While people in the North are watching a display of northern lights, a mirror-image array of southern lights is flickering above the heads of penguins in Antarctica. Day and night, summer and winter, auroras cavort above the Earth at heights of one hundred to one thousand kilometers (sixty to six hundred miles). Powered by particles from the sun, shaped by the Earth's magnetic field, and colored by gases in the upper atmosphere, they bear witness to the immense, invisible processes that animate our home region of the universe.

WATCHING THE SHOW

We are used to thinking of the aurora as capricious and wild, endlessly inventive. But in the past few years, it has become apparent that the behavior of the auroral ovals is constrained within certain limits. Thus, while every brilliant aurora has its unique runs and riffs, these are best understood as free improvisations on a standard progression. That progression—the stages the aurora goes through as it develops and fades—is known to science as the auroral substorm.

Although substorms (like so much else) were first described by Norwegian scientist Kristian Birkeland (1867–1917), they were first documented in 1964 by Syun-Ichi Akasofu of the University of Alaska, using series of all-sky photographs and, later, imagery from spacecraft. For an observer on the ground, a typical substorm begins in the late evening hours with quiet auroral curtains that lie along the horizon. After a while, the lights brighten, and distinct streaks, or rays, appear in the glow. Soon a series of large, sweeping folds or spirals form, beginning near the eastern horizon and surging rapidly west-ward. This lovely spectacle is sometimes known as an auroral breakup, by analogy with the dramatic springtime release of ice from northern rivers.

The development of this westward-traveling surge marks the beginning of the so-called expansion phase of the substorm. It is followed, near midnight, by another outburst, in which the aurora suddenly brightens and then breaks into a wild fandango of swirling movement. After a few minutes of this, the scene gradually quiets down and the aurora resumes its demure appearance. This is the beginning of the recovery phase, in the early-morning hours, when the discrete forms disappear and are replaced by a vague, diffuse haze that resembles thin cloud. These clouds soon begin to flash on and off, in a display of power that is less spectacular than what has gone before, but no less awesome. From beginning to end, a substorm lasts from one to three hours. This process can be observed somewhere on Earth at least once every twenty-four hours.

Scientists are still debating what it is that triggers these regular, patterned outbursts. Some believe that substorms are controlled by processes entirely within the magnetotail, a trailing extension of the Earth's magnetic field. According to this theory, the Earth's magnetic field can be likened to a leaky bucket that is constantly taking in energy from the solar wind, the stream of high-energy particles that is thrown off by the sun. Once trapped by the Earth's magnetic field, some of this energy leaks away in a continual drizzle of electrons that maintain the aurora in its quiet state. But as energy continues to pour in from the solar wind, the bucket goes on filling until, suddenly, it reaches its limit, overturns, and floods its contents into the atmosphere. This massive influx of electrons and energy causes a substorm.

Others believe (with increasingly good evidence) that substorms are not just caused by changes within the magnetotail but are also triggered directly by the solar wind. To extend the metaphor, it is as if the leaky bucket were held by a giant. When the giant is stung by a bee—in this case, a jab of energy from the solar wind—he loses his equilibrium and out spills the energy. To rephrase this description in more technical language, a substorm appears to be an impulsive, nonlinear response to subtle changes in the strength, polarity, and angle of solar-wind magnetism.

Substorms are just one of the ways in which the aurora responds to the solar wind. Dramatic auroral displays tend to occur at intervals of twenty-seven days, just the time it takes for the sun to rotate once, relative to the Earth. This is because of features on the sun known as coronal holes—openings in the sun's magnetic field through which strong gusts of solar wind shoot out. When one of these blasts nears the Earth, the auroral machine goes on Red Alert. Extra energy surges into the magnetotail and through the auroral circuits, causing substorms to become more frequent, more active, and more beautiful. At the same time, the auroral ovals expand toward the equator, bringing their splendor to audiences in more temperate latitudes. This may continue for several days and nights, until the coronal hole rotates away from us and sends its jet of particles into empty space. On the next rotation, the blast hits us again; and then again and again, until the hole fades away.

The ability of the auroral ovals to change size—to expand and contract—is one of their most remarkable characteristics. They are like doughnut-shaped bubbles, quivering in the breeze, constantly teased and tickled by the changing winds of solar activity. When the solar wind is relatively quiet, the auroral bubbles hover placidly around the poles, experiencing brief orgasmic spasms when a substorm occurs. But when the wind is fierce, the ovals are rippled with storms as they swell and spread toward the equator. Any time auroras are seen at mid-latitudes, it is a sign the sun is hitting us with a blast of solar wind. For example, the ovals tend to enlarge in the spring and fall because the Earth is then seasonally tilted toward the outer margins of the sun—the regions where coronal holes are most likely to occur.

And what about sunspots? Do sunspots also enhance the flow of the solar wind? Is that why their numbers correlate, more or less, with reports of dramatic auroras? The present-day answer is (as you might expect) intriguingly convoluted. In the first place, it turns out that sunspots are not themselves sources of solar wind. Instead, they are areas of intense magnetism that actually hold the particles in. But even though sunspots do not release solar wind, they are associated with other structures that do. Both result from chaotic movements in the core of the sun, which work up to peak intensity about once in eleven years. When the core builds to full boil, sunspots become larger and more numerous, and the magnetic fields within them get twisted and stretched. They are like powerful, tightly wound springs, stressed to the breaking point. Sooner or later, the tension explodes in a fiery prominence, or solar flare, which usually erupts in the region near a large group of spots. As the explosion belches forth tongues of fire, it hurtles gale-force plasma into the solar system.

When this hurricane hits the Earth's field a few days later, power charges through the auroral circuits. As the auroral ovals receive this surge, they overflow their usual bounds and flood both south and north toward the equator. Strong substorms hit one after the other, filling the skies with their brilliant theatrics. Under exceptional circumstances, high red-oxygen aurora may also develop at these times and wrap the globe in a blaze of crimson.

And so you have it, at least in broad outline—the space-age understanding of the polar lights. While some aspects of the process remain obscure (the exact nature of the solar-wind/Earth dynamo, the structure of the electron accelerator above the auroral curtains, the physics of a substorm), the basic picture is beyond dispute. We have been up there with our cameras and instruments. We have collected "ocular proof" to support our theories. Whatever revisions the future may judge necessary, we know that many age-old questions have received answers.

But at the same time we know that our questions about the aurora can never be put to rest. The aurora is not just a puzzle to solve; it is also a mystery to experience. We cannot account for the miracle of a leaf through biochemistry nor explain a human child through developmental theory. Why should we expect to still the aurora with physics and mathematics? For even if we could account, minute by minute, for every fold and flicker of light, we would not have it all. We would know *how* the aurora is formed, but nothing can tell us *why*. Why has our home planet, Earth, been graced with this glory? And why have our minds always been tuned to watch it in awe?

HITS

and Misses

SKUNKED

*Keeping Peace
with the Neighbors*

here I come from in Saskatchewan, people shoot skunks on sight. It is, as someone reminded me the other day, "a farmer thing to do." So I wasn't surprised when my new country neighbor steamed up to announce that "we" had a skunk problem. The night before, she and her husband had killed a family of three—"a mother and two babies"—by the slough that separates our yards. "I thought you should know," she said. "We're doing our best." And, as abruptly as she'd appeared, she sped off again.

I'm a newcomer here, a weekender whose connection to rural life is admittedly whimsical. For no very good reason, I had recently become co-owner of a charming and uninhabitable country church, whose shiny onion domes were now veiled in the swirling dust of my neighbor's departure. Truth to tell, she'd left me in a cloud as well. To fit into this community meant becoming a skunk-killer?

Skunks can be a nuisance. Oh, all right, they can be appalling, eye-watering, stomach-turning pests. I've often wondered what I would do if my amiable but bumbling golden retriever (three-time western Canadian porcupine-chasing champ) had chosen to add them to her list of acquaintances. Surely, my new neighbors could be forgiven for wanting rid of them?

Skunk-bashing is a venerable tradition Canada. The first written description I can find, published in 1686, casts skunks out of creation as *"les enfants du diable,"* children of the devil. According to historian F. Gabriel Sagard-Théodat, author of this account, these dismal beasts were not only "of very bad odour" but were also ugly and mean. What's more, they were said to excrete "little serpents" which had the sole virtue of dying quickly.

The bad reputation of the skunk is with us still, sustained in large part by half-truths and exaggeration. Out west, for example, everybody "knows" that skunks carry disease. It is true that rabies is always present in the skunk population of the prairies. But a call to the Canadian Food Inspection Agency's rabies unit in Lethbridge, Alberta, quickly ascertained that there is not exactly an emergency around here. No rabid skunk has been reported in west-central Saskatchewan for many years, although the overall number of cases in western Canada does appear to be on the rise. Reason enough for caution; reason enough to make sure that our dogs and cats get regular rabies shots. But surely not reason to kill every skunk that ambles across the lawn.

Pace Sagard-Théodat, healthy skunks are peaceable, not mean-spirited. Short-sighted and self-absorbed, they snuffle along, mostly at night, in search of small prey such as grasshoppers and voles. This diet of vermin might earn them a place on a list of Humankind's Best Friends were it not for their stellar evolutionary achievement—and chief offense. Skunks have mastered the art of chemical self-defense. Yet they are not walking stench dispensers, just waiting to let fly. Their lives depend on their noxious spray, and to them it is as precious as Chanel No. 5. As biologist and skunk researcher Serge Larivière puts it, "They only have a few shots at a time, and when it's gone, they have no other way to defend themselves. They're dead." Since skunk musk is deadly in its own way, one shot will usually suffice. But why spend even that if it is not required? Larivière devoted three summers to tracking radio-collared skunks through the wilds of Saskatchewan, without incident, documenting the animal's warning displays. A sequence of escalating behaviors—tail up, stomp, hiss, charge, scratch, and aim—almost always precedes a direct hit. If Fido is too dense to take the hint, perhaps she deserves what comes next.

When Larivière describes skunks, he uses words like "interesting," "efficient," and "misunderstood." "People think skunks stink, run around aimlessly, and are stupid. They shoot them without knowing why." It's all wrong—but what's right? What can my neighbors and I do to keep skunks out of town? For a start, Larivière suggests that we get busy right away, boarding up vacant buildings and spaces that could serve as homes for skunks. The ideal time to do this is around 1:00 A.M. some night between mid-July, when the kits are old enough to leave their natal dens, and the end of August, when young and old alike will begin to seek shelter for the coming months. Skunks bed down for winter en masse—one male with up to twenty willing consorts—so shutting down even one such site may solve the problem at the source. Not even a city slicker could raise a stink about that.

SAVING MOOSE
BY FEEDING BEARS

Manna from Heaven

*I*n east-central Alaska, near the Yukon border, it rained moose for two months, on and off, in the spring of 1985. Train-killed moose—twelve tonnes, or tons, in all. The last the animals knew, they had been ambling down the railroad tracks, unaware of their onrushing doom. Soon their remains were being ferried aloft by chopper and flung into the muskeg and hills around the Mosquito Fork River.

The airdrops had been orchestrated by Rod Boertje and his colleagues from the Alaska Department of Fish and Game in an attempt to figure out what, apart from oncoming freights, was causing problems for the local moose. Not that the animals were endangered or even in decline. In fact, since their numbers had bottomed out in the mid-1970s, the counts had been remarkably stable. Stable and low. And that, for biologists charged with creating opportunities for moose hunting, was a problem in itself. If this region could theoretically support up to twelve hundred moose on 1,000 square kilometers (about 400 square miles), why had the animals spent a decade at densities of sixty or one hundred? Everything had seemed in their favor: decent weather, abundant browse, restricted hunting, low wolf predation. Yet the population was stuck in the cellar. What was going on?

The very first season of research, 1984, provided a promising lead. Although the region supported few wolves, it turned out to have a thriving population of grizzlies, which subsisted mainly on a monkish regime of roots and berries. But during moose calving season, the bears indulged in an orgy of meat-eating. Of thirty-three newborn moose radio-collared that year, seventeen were eaten by grizzlies.

And so it happened, in the spring of the following year, that the researchers decided to rain train-struck moose meat into the calving grounds. The idea was simple: the carcasses would serve as bait for grizzlies, which could then be caught and radio-collared so that their diet could be monitored. Again, the results were unambiguous. Grizzlies were keeping the moose population in a "pit" by feasting on calves during their vulnerable first weeks.

In reporting their research in the *Canadian Journal of Zoology,* Boertje and his group drew the only possible conclusion. To boost the moose in this system, you would have to "remove" predators. What else to do with a problem bear except kill it?

But was this really the only choice? As the study progressed, the biologists began to notice a strange blip in their graphs. Usually, when they checked the moose in early winter, they found just one cow in ten traveling with young. But in 1985, every second cow they saw was followed closely by a calf.

As Boertje and his colleagues pondered this unexpected good news, they began to wonder if the upturn might be a result of their own efforts. There was, after all, the small matter of 12,000 kilograms (about 26,000 pounds) of meat that had fallen, like manna from heaven, into the paths of bears and wolves that spring. Could this supplementary feeding—much of it provided, by chance, when the moose were giving birth—have diverted grizzlies and other predators from the tender young calves?

Five years later, Boertje was finally able to put the idea to the test, this time freighting 26,000 kilograms (57,000 pounds) of roadkill into his research block at peak calving time. That winter's cow/calf ratio was the highest in nine years and up to four times better than anywhere else in the region. "Diversionary feeding" had worked.

Who would have thought it? After generations of numbly killing predators, convinced that there were no alternatives, it turned out that *feeding* them might produce the results biologists were seeking.

Recently, wildlife managers in the cattle country of southwestern Alberta began using a variation on this technique to help reduce grizzly predation during calving. Their strategy was to "redistribute" the carcasses of road-killed deer by collecting them from rangelands in the valleys and airlifting them up into the foothills. As the grizzlies roused from hibernation and wandered downslope in the spring, they encountered the smorgasbord of carcasses that had been laid out for them, well away from the temptations of the pastures. Only one cow was taken by a grizzly (down from double-digit losses most years), and the bears went on their way with minimal interference.

"We were really going against the grain on this," admits biologist Richard Quinlan of Alberta's Natural Resources Service. "But so far it's all been really positive."

Our traditional confrontation with predators is literally a dead end, a joyless, repetitive routine of violence that wastes the lives of thousands of bears each year. In British Columbia alone, conservation officers shot 35 grizzlies and 1,619 black bears as "problems" in 1998. "Diversionary feeding" is no teddy bears' picnic in which things always end well. Yet it stands as a welcome reminder that an oddball new idea can turn our thinking on its head, revealing possibilities we had scarcely imagined.

RULE OF THE WOLF

Restoring Order to
Yellowstone National Park

*T*he raven does a double take, circles back, and cranes its neck for a better look. For a long moment, it hangs over our heads, as if trying to make sense of the strange spectacle on the trail below. This is what it sees. Half a dozen people are proceeding slowly down a narrow, stone-walled valley in Yellowstone National Park, our boots and skis chattering against the ice-glazed snow of mid-March. In the center of our group, on an orange plastic sled, lies the body of a wolf. Big, once bold, still beautiful. Dead.

There was a time, not so very long ago, when humans hunted wolves to extinction not only here in Yellowstone, the world's first national park, but across much of the continent, from central Canada south through the United States to the Mexican highlands. As recently as the late 1920s, when the last of Yellowstone's native wolf population was eliminated from the Lamar River valley, just down the road, the sight of a dead wolf was cause for raucous joy. In those days, the animals were reviled as bloodthirsty killers, nature red in tooth and claw, the enemies of progress and civilization. But the procession on the trail today is not jubilant. The laughter that ripples up from our conversations is quiet; our pace is respectful. A whole new conception of the wolf lies bundled on that sled, a vision of a species that not only takes life but also, unexpectedly, gives it.

Overhead, the raven is still hoping to claim that gift of life for itself. After feeding on wolf-killed elk all winter, will this be an opportunity to feed on the hunter as well? We pause to watch as the would-be scavenger loops above us, stark against silver-gray clouds, and then drifts over a cliff and away from the threat of human presence. It will have another chance. Wolves are back in Yellowstone—to stay this time—and they have set the whole place buzzing with opportunity and surprise.

THE PLAN

The task of overseeing the reintroduction of wolves into Yellowstone—and of assessing the complex ways in which they are making their presence felt—has fallen to Douglas Smith, a tall, rangy biologist with a goofy handlebar moustache and chiseled good looks. It was Smith who first picked up the insistent beeping of the dead wolf's radio collar and then organized a crew to ski into the mountains and retrieve its carcass. Later, with the wolf on its way for a post-mortem, he and I reconvene in his book-lined cubbyhole of an office at park headquarters in Mammoth Hot Springs, Wyoming.

Now in his forties, with hair that is tending to wolf-gray at the temples, Smith has been with the Yellowstone Wolf Project since its inception in November 1994. That winter, fourteen wolves from a flourishing population near Hinton, Alberta, were trucked into the park, held briefly in acclimation pens, then sent forth to make a new life in a new land. That first release was followed a year later by the introduction of an additional seventeen animals from Pink Mountain near Fort St. John, British Columbia—the ancestors of the unfortunate wolf we dragged down the mountain. Turned loose into a carnivore's paradise of bison and elk, with no resident wolf packs to hold them back, the pioneering population experienced such exuberant growth that planned introductions for succeeding years were cancelled. "We were ahead of schedule and under budget back then," recalls Smith, cracking a grin. "Everybody liked that."

The immediate goal of the program was to establish at least 10 resident packs of wolves in the park and its surrounding public and private lands, an area known as the Greater Yellowstone Ecosystem and, at 73,000 square kilometers (28,000 square miles), just slightly smaller than New Brunswick. By 2003, the objective was long surpassed, with a population that appeared to be leveling out at about 31 packs, with 19 breeding pairs and more than 250 adults. In part because of this historic achievement, the U.S. Fish and Wildlife Service recently nudged gray wolves down one step on its list of species at risk, from "endangered" to merely "threatened" in most of the contiguous forty-eight states.

AN ACT OF HEALING

"The reintroduction of gray wolves into Yellowstone has to rank as one of the most important acts of wildlife conservation in the last century," says Smith, his faded blue eyes suddenly intense. "This is an act of healing, the restoration of one of the last great ecosystems on the planet."

Hold it right there. An act of healing? How can a killer such as the wolf heal anything? Consider, for example, what has happened to the wolf's smaller cousin, the coyote, in the northern range of the park. Apparently scarce before wolves were wiped out, coyotes prospered mightily in their absence. In the mid-1990s, just before the wolf reintroduction program, no fewer than eighty coyotes in twelve packs—the densest population ever known—were roaming through the wide, flowing reaches of the Lamar River valley, where they feasted on rodents, winter-killed ungulates, and elk calves. By 1998, this robust population had been reduced to thirty-six survivors in nine small packs. That's a violent loss of more than 50 percent in just three years. Although the coyote population has since stabilized, as the underdogs learn how to keep out of harm's way, they are still brutally excluded from the core-use areas of wolf territories. Where's the healing in that?

Smith would be the first to admit that wolves are killers—"good, effective killers." But he hastens to add that killing, whether in the form of predation or dog-on-dog conflict, can be a natural and constructive force. In this case, for instance, the absence of a top predator for sixty-odd years had allowed coyotes to rise to such extreme abundance that the entire ecosystem had been thrown out of whack. As evidence, he points to coyote research done by the husband-and-wife team of Bob Crabtree and Jennifer Sheldon, who found that at their peak, coyotes on Yellowstone's northern range were taking an enormous bite out of the local rodent population. In any given year, something like a quarter of all pocket gophers, a third of the ground squirrels, and two-thirds of voles were disappearing into the coyotes' jaws.

"What did that do to all the other rodent predators?" asks Smith, rhetorically. Although a study of rodent numbers has not yet been finalized, early results suggest that ground squirrels have increased explosively since wolves were reintroduced, particularly in the core areas, where coyotes no longer dare set foot. (Farley Mowat's *Never Cry Wolf* notwithstanding, Yellowstone wolves feed primarily on elk, not on rodents.) By trimming back the coyote population—and giving rodent numbers a chance to increase—wolves have almost certainly opened up opportunities for foxes, raptors, and other rodent hunters.

And that's just the beginning. A group Smith calls the "scavenger guild," varied freeloaders that feed on wolf kills, is enjoying an even bigger bonanza. Smith's arithmetic is persuasive. Let's say, for example, that a pack of wolves takes down a cow elk, at an average weight of 200 to 225 kilograms (450 to 500 pounds). If a wolf's stomach can hold 10 kilograms (20 pounds) of meat and there are ten animals in the pack, that means they can chow down only half the carcass at a time. And when the hunters are bedded down, sleeping off their excess, in come the scavengers—bald and golden eagles, magpies, ravens, foxes, coyotes, black and grizzly bears—to steal as much of the banquet as they can.

"We've seen a grizzly emerge from hibernation in late winter and make a beeline straight to a wolf kill," Smith says. And ravens are even more spectacularly attentive. Smith's right-hand man on the wolf project, Dan Stahler, came to Yellowstone as a master's student in 1998, specifically to study the relationship between wolves and ravens. His conclusion: ravens are called "wolf-birds" for good reason. Of twenty-nine wolf kills he observed in the course of his research, ravens not only found every single one but found them fast—within four minutes of the time of death. By contrast, the birds located only a third of the carcasses that Stahler set out himself, and they didn't land

and feed on any of them. It was obvious to him that the birds were purposefully following wolves and waiting for them to kill in order to be first in line to grab a bellyful. On one memorable occasion, Stahler counted 135 ravens at a wolf kill.

"Every year, I find new nests," says Stahler gleefully, "places I've never found them before. I can't prove it, but I'm pretty sure there are more ravens than there were before the wolves returned." And if more ravens, then more grizzlies? More eagles and magpies? Perhaps more wolverines? By inadvertently providing sustenance to meat-eaters large and small, wolves are sending a pulse of energy through the ecological web and bringing the Yellowstone landscape back to vibrant health.

COMPETING INTERESTS

Smith is keenly aware there are people who mistrust this line of sensitive New Age talk. They're the guys in ball caps and Stetsons who accost him at public meetings, call him a liar, threaten to kill his dog, or sneer that he's "a government pig at the taxpayers' trough." Still deeply imbued with the old view of the wolf as a black-hearted fiend, these folks—who speak for a dominant, though by no means universal, segment of rural society—aren't easily impressed by arguments about ripple effects and biodiversity. For them, the matter is simple. True, wolves haven't killed as many cattle as people predicted at first, but they are carrying out a wholesale slaughter of Yellowstone's northern-range elk, and something has to be done about it.

At first glance, the numbers appear to speak for themselves. In the mid-1990s, before the reintroduction began, the northern Yellowstone elk herd stood at around seventeen thousand head, just down from an all-time high a year earlier of nineteen thousand. Since then, with wolves back in action, the population has been wavering downward toward an average of ten thousand to twelve thousand animals. "A lot of people who hate wolves, and I mean literally hate them, have said that the difference between those two numbers is wolves and only wolves," Smith laments. "It's my facts against their facts."

Unlike his opponents, Smith takes into account the dynamics of a free-ranging herd in a free and dynamic world. As he sees it, the population spike of the early 1990s probably represented an unhealthy extreme that pushed the elk beyond the carrying capacity of their range. "Being at a historic, all-time high, there wasn't much the elk could do except take a downturn." In addition, he points to the effects of a severe six-year drought that has reduced much of the northern range to the driest conditions this past century. "We're getting signs that a lack of food is starting to affect the elk," Smith says. So while wolves have undoubtedly played a role in the decline of the northern herd, they are only one small part of a large and complex picture.

But what really makes Smith's blood boil is the still-too-common belief that wolves are unstoppable, invincible killing machines. "It's just not true," he says. "All things being equal, wolves cannot kill healthy, mature elk. It just ain't gonna happen." Of 743 kills that Smith and his team have examined on the northern range, only 11 percent represented elk in the prime years of life, between ages one and nine. The remaining victims were all either young and defenseless or old and decrepit. Wolves are simply not able to run riot through the herd, taking down healthy animals at random.

Smith likens the relationship between wolves and elk to an evolutionary arms race in which the opposing forces advance, step-by-step, so that attack is always countered by defense. "What people overestimate is the ability of wolves to kill," he says. "What they underestimate is the tactical defense of elk." Some three hundred wolves have so far been radio-collared by the wolf project, of which seven or eight have been killed by prey. The dead wolf we hauled down the mountain had bled from the mouth, as if it had suffered the same fate, though a post-mortem eventually concluded that it died of an unspecified disease.

THE RIPPLE EFFECT

Although wolves are not going to decimate the elk population, they do definitely affect the animals' behavior in subtle yet significant ways. Recent work by two researchers at the University of Alberta in Edmonton, graduate student Julie Mao and her supervisor Mark Boyce, strongly suggests that the elk are shifting away from areas within Yellowstone where wolves have the greatest presence. By comparing thousands of coordinates from radio-collared elk, both pre- and post-wolf, Mao and Boyce have shown that the animals are now spending their summers higher in the mountains, on steeper slopes, and in deeper forest than they did before the wolves returned. "This is consistent with the idea," says Boyce, "that the elk are moving away from the valley bottoms where the wolves have their dens."

Who really cares where elk spend their time? Doug Smith does, for one. To him, this shift in elk behavior signals the beginning of a process of change that will bring new life and variety to the entire northern range. If elk move out of the valleys, he reasons, this will give a breather to the stands of willow and aspen around low-lying wetlands and creeks, which are now being denuded by heavy browsing. If the trees have a chance to regenerate, they will provide habitat for animals and birds that are currently rare or missing from the local ecosystem. Birds such as yellow warblers and willow flycatchers. Animals like beavers.

"This is the hottest arena in science right now," Smith says happily. "I know of at least five teams of researchers who all hope to be first to prove that there are more willows in Yellowstone because there are wolves." Contenders for the willow crown include the University of Alberta's Mark Boyce, colleague Evelyn Merrill, and student Nathan Varley, who are attacking the problem with high-tech, aerial video-imaging. Smith is certain that the transformation is already afoot. In 2000, in his secondary role as Yellowstone's beaver expert, he located four new colonies of the willow-chewing rodents in the northeastern corner of the park, in an area where willows were rare and beavers had long been absent.

"I always tell people, come back to Yellowstone in twenty-five or thirty years, and the place will look different," he says. "You might see ponds with luxurious willows and sapling aspens, with beavers and willow flycatchers, warblers, muskrats, mink—even otters, animals that are very rare now. And that difference will be due to wolves." Smith describes wolves as a keystone species, animals that, though comparatively rare themselves, bring diversity and richness and balance to the world around them. This is the lesson of the Yellowstone Wolf Project and a message that holds true on either side of the forty-ninth parallel. In return for providing wolves for reintroduction, Canadians have been offered a profound new vision of the relationship between life and death and a new conception of wolves, wherever we have the good fortune to find them.

CARIBOU

STAKES

Gambling for Arctic Oil

*E*very April, a pulse of life surges through the spruce forests of the north-central Yukon and the far western Northwest Territories. All winter long, the frozen region has provided quiet refuge for thousands of caribou, including many of the 129,000-strong Porcupine caribou herd *(Rangifer tarandus granti)*. For months, the animals have lived minimally: resting, walking slowly, pawing through snow for food, enduring the elements.

But come spring—the season of birth—the herd is suddenly overtaken by an urgent desire to travel. With pregnant cows in the vanguard, they head to the north and west, following the grain of the Richardson Mountains, forging across swollen streams, and eventually trotting lightly over the invisible line that separates Canada from the United States.

As a rule, most of the caribou funnel onto a narrow strip of lowlands along the Alaska coast. Here, as the cotton-grass flowers push up through late spring drifts, as many as fifty thousand caribou cows give birth.

The Porcupine caribou have returned to these calving grounds for untold thousands of years, following a lifeway that keeps time with the energy of the seasons. But they soon may face an intrusion by outsiders whose energy demands have spiraled out of control—an industrial landscape of drilling platforms, oil wells, pipelines, and roads. At least, that is the vision of one George W. Bush. President Bush, a former Texas oilman, argues that America's national security is jeopardized by its dependence on foreign energy, and he has committed himself to boosting U.S. domestic production of oil and gas. According to recent estimates, this calving ground and its environs may contain up to 16 billion barrels of oil, of which anywhere from 1.9 billion to 9.4 billion barrels are "economically recoverable." Given that Americans use 7 billion barrels of oil a year, this is a drop in the bucket, but it is a drop that the Bush administration is eager to extract.

ZEROING IN ON TEN-OH-TWO

Strictly speaking, the calving grounds fall within the boundaries of the Arctic National Wildlife Refuge, a protected zone of some 7.7 million hectares (30,000 square miles) in the northeast corner of Alaska. Established in 1960, the refuge was doubled to its present size about twenty years ago, against vociferous opposition from oil and gas interests. Although most of the reserve was designated as wilderness at that time, the issue of the 608,000-hectare (2,300-square-mile) coastal plain—including the oil-rich calving grounds—proved so contentious that it had to be set aside. The status of this area was left unresolved under Section 1002 of the Alaska National

Interest Land Conservation Act (1980), pending an assessment of the effects of oil production on Arctic wildlife. It is this so-called Ten-Oh-Two Area that President Bush has pledged to open to the oil industry.

Proponents of oil production on the 1002 lands insist that development can proceed without posing a threat to the Porcupine herd. As evidence, they point to the experience of the Central Arctic herd, which has shared its calving grounds with an oil field for almost thirty years. When development began around Prudhoe Bay in Alaska in the mid-1970s, the population of the Central Arctic herd stood at a meager 5,000 to 6,000. Since then, despite a manic proliferation of pipelines and roads, the population has increased to 27,000. In the view of Alaska senator Frank Murkowski, a similarly bright future awaits the Porcupine herd if development goes ahead. As he assures the world on his website, "The fear that Arctic development will harm the caribou [is] groundless."

SIGNS OF STRESS

But Don Russell, manager of the Canadian Wildlife Service in the Yukon and Canada's leading expert on the Porcupine herd, thinks Murkowski is too sanguine. "In spite of its success," he says, "the Central Arctic herd has paid a significant price for development." He compares its fivefold increase with a simultaneous sevenfold advance made by the neighboring Teshekpuk Lake caribou herd, which has been spared the stress of development. Perhaps, says Russell, this gap begins to represent the biological cost of Prudhoe Bay oil.

A patient, soft-spoken man, Russell measures his words, careful to stay within the boundaries of what he and his colleagues have learned during nearly thirty years of research.

"Caribou are an adaptable species that have some ability to cope with human activity," he says. "But calving caribou in particular do not like development."

Alaskan biologist Scott Wolfe recently confirmed this conclusion. Wolfe's research demonstrates that between 1980 and 1995, cows in the Central Arctic herd shifted their calving away from the industrialized features of Prudhoe Bay and the nearby Kuparuk oil field. Instead, they began bearing calves in low-quality habitat outside the development zone, even though it meant abandoning patches of richer vegetation that benefit lactation. How this is affecting calf survival and the caribou's long-term productivity remains unknown, but it cannot be doing the herd any good.

The same kinds of disruptions could be expected if development proceeds on the Porcupine herd's calving grounds, says Russell, but likely with more serious effects. The Central Arctic herd has access to a broad coastal plain about 150 kilometers (90 miles) across, much of which provides more-or-less adequate habitat for calving. By contrast, the Porcupine herd's calving ground is only about 20 kilometers (12 miles) wide. If the animals are disturbed, there is no obvious place for them to go.

There are also worrying signs that the Porcupine herd is already under stress from another concomitant of our runaway appetite for oil and gas. Over the past three decades, average spring temperatures in the northern Yukon have increased by an incredible six degrees Celsius (eleven degrees Fahrenheit). As a result, the caribou are calving farther north, a trend that increases their already heavy reliance on the 1002 lands. Sixty percent of the herd's calves are born on the coastal plain, double what it was in the 1980s.

Other effects of climate change have the potential to be equally worrying but are harder to document. Through the 1980s, the Porcupine caribou shared in the upward surge that buoyed the numbers of the Central Arctic herd and other caribou populations throughout the North. But since 1989, the Porcupine herd has settled into a steady downward trend, declining at a rate of 3 to 4 percent a year. Just why this is happening is not clear. There has been no obvious increase in predation or hunting. The latter has been maintained at a steady 2 to 3 percent, most of it a subsistence hunt by the Vuntut Gwich'in First Nation of Old Crow, Yukon.

The obvious reasons for such a decline, such as low productivity, poor calf survival, or high adult mortality, have been eliminated. The cows are still producing plenty of calves. So attention has focused on global warming. The rise in spring temperatures may be changing conditions along the migration route in ways that make life difficult for caribou. For example, prematurely soggy snow might force the animals up onto windswept ridge tops, where they are easier prey for wolves. Even when things are going well, "the Porcupine herd has the lowest rate of productivity of any barren ground caribou herd we know," Russell says. "It doesn't take very much added mortality or stress to turn a population increase into a loss."

Given that the herd is already experiencing difficulties, the last thing it needs is disturbance during calving. Russell's voice takes on an uncharacteristic edge as he summarizes the likely impact of the proposed oil development on the Porcupine caribou. "If you wanted to undertake activity," he says, "you probably couldn't think of a worse place to do it or a worse time of year or a worse herd of caribou to do it to."

THE FIGHT GOES ON

The Canadian government strongly echoes Russell's concern. "We support responsible development in habitats that are not critical," says Foreign Affairs spokesperson Reynald Doiron, "but experts in the field inform us that the calving ground is critical for the Porcupine herd. We hope and expect that the Americans will give permanent protection to 1002."

The development lobby, even with President Bush's backing, is in for a fight. Aligned in opposition are the Porcupine Caribou Management Board, the Vuntut Gwich'in First Nation, almost every major conservation organization on the continent, including the Canadian Parks and Wilderness Society, the Canadian Nature Federation, Greenpeace, the Sierra Club, the Wilderness Society, and the World Wildlife Fund, and, of course, the Canadian government.

On February 26, 2001, Senator Murkowski and Senator John Breaux introduced the National Energy Security Act, which contains provisions to allow drilling on 1002 lands. In 1995, a similar measure was approved by the House of Representatives and the Senate but was vetoed by President Clinton. No last-minute reprieve is expected from President Bush.

The Murkowski/Breaux bill died in the Senate in 2001. Since then, the Bush administration has attempted to force the issue through the Senate and the House of Representatives by including it in must-pass budget bills, so far without success. Despite these delays, both Bush and Murkowski — now governor of Alaska — remain committed to getting their hands on the 1002 lands.

STAYING

Alive

STUCK ON
THE PRAIRIES

Where Is Here?

here are people who think of
the prairie as boring, and it is
hard not to pity them. We see them on the highways, trapped
inside their cars, propelled by a burning desire to be somewhere else. But even as we wonder at their hurry, we have to
admit that these disgruntled travelers are following in a grand
old North American tradition. On both sides of the Canada–
U.S. border, prairie bashing is as old as the written record. In
1803, for example, when the United States was contemplating
the acquisition of the lands west of the Mississippi River from
the French, through the Louisiana Purchase, the great orator
Daniel Webster was moved to object. "What do we want with
this vast, worthless area," he thundered, "this region of savages
and wild beasts, of deserts of shifting sands and whirlwinds of
dust, of cactus and prairie dogs?" And even after this suppos-
edly howling wilderness had been annexed to the U.S., many
observers remained unimpressed. The painter and naturalist

John James Audubon was among them. In 1843, we find him traveling up the Missouri River on his first visit to the Great Plains. Forced onto the shore when his steamboat became grounded on a sandbar, he turned a disparaging eye toward the Dakota countryside. "The prairies around us are the most arid and dismal you can conceive of," he wrote. "In fact these prairies (so called) look more like great deserts."

Another traveler of the same era, a trader named Rufus Sage, was even more direct: "That this section of the country should ever become inhabited by civilized man except in the vicinity of large water courses, is an idea too preposterous to be entertained for a single moment." North of the border, Captain John Palliser, who crossed the Saskatchewan prairies in the late 1850s, was of much the same mind. Forget farming, he recommended. This country is just too dry.

It wasn't until near the end of the nineteenth century that the tide of expert opinion turned and the Great Plains were opened to agricultural settlement, now touted far and wide as the new Garden of Eden. The fact was, however, that these magnificent grasslands were neither desert nor garden but something completely new to European and Euro-American experience. So new that at first there wasn't even a name for them in either French or English. Pressed to come up with something, the early French fur traders had extended their term for a woodland meadow—*une prairie*—as a kind of metaphor for this big, wide, sparsely wooded, windswept world. But the Great Plains were far more than a meadow. What the travelers had encountered was a vast, dynamic ecosystem, a kind of tawny, slowly evolving organism that, in a climate of constant change, had sustained itself ever since the retreat of the glaciers at the end of the Ice Age. In the presence of this strangeness and grandeur, words and vision failed.

When the newcomers looked around them, all they could see was where they weren't. This was not forest or sea coast or mountains; it was nothing but light and grass, the Big Empty in the middle of the continent. A vacant space, as they saw it, in desperate need of improvement. And this failure of vision—this inability to see and appreciate the Great Plains grasslands for what they truly are—has continued to plague our perceptions right down to the present. Flat? Boring? Lifeless? Nothing could be further from the truth. It's time to drop out of the fast lane and give the prairies, our prairies, a second, loving look.

AN EMPIRE OF GRASS

The key to everything that happens on the prairies lies trampled under our feet. Although grasses may look humble, they are actually versatile and tough, capable of growing under the widest possible range of conditions. Anywhere plants can grow, grasses are likely to be on the scene, whether coexisting with cactuses in a desert, poking up among lichens on the Arctic tundra, or hiding in the leafy understory of a forest. And when circumstances are especially favorable for them—for example, when the climate strikes just the right balance between precipitation and drought—grasses can assert themselves to become the dominant vegetation. ("Dominance," in this case, refers to the plants that contribute the most living tissue, or biomass, to the ecosystem. As trees to forest, so grasses to grasslands.)

A glance at a map of the world's major grasslands suggests that these conditions are most likely to occur on a broad, landlocked plain, far from any significant body of water, somewhere near the center of a continental landmass. It is in this semiarid environment—too wet to be a desert and too dry for forest—that grasses gain the upper hand, whether it be on the

steppes of central Asia, on the pampas of Argentina, on the savannas of East Africa, or in the broad heartland of North
America.

Globally, grasslands are the largest of the four terrestrial
biomes, or life zones, with a sweep that extends across roughly
one-quarter of the land area of the planet, more than tundra,
desert, or woodlands. (At least, that's the area over which
grasses would potentially hold sway if natural conditions were
allowed to prevail.) We're talking some 46 million square kilometers (18 million square miles)—almost three times the area
of Russia. In North America alone, grasslands naturally extend
over about 3.5 million square kilometers (1.4 million square
miles), an area larger than many of the world's major nations.

The first European known to have set foot on this great em-
pire of grass was a soldier and sometime explorer named Francisco Vásquez de Coronado. Dispatched from Mexico City in
1540, he was supposed to investigate rumors about a kingdom
called Cíbola, somewhere to the north, and to plunder its
Seven Cities of Gold. When these glittering mirages turned
out to be sun-baked Zuñi pueblos in what is now New Mexico,
he turned his attention to the uncharted Great Plains, where
the fish were as big as horses, the people ate off golden plates,
and the king was lulled to sleep at night by a tree full of
golden bells. At least that's what people told him and what he
chose to believe. And so off set Coronado, with a party of
armed men, in the vague direction of present-day Kansas. In
the end the promised golden city turned out to be a village of
grass-thatched huts, where the people lived by hunting bison
and growing gardens, each in their season.

Yet despite this disillusionment, Coronado and his party
were astonished by what they found along their route. Here

lay "a wilderness in which nothing grew, except for very small plants," but which nonetheless was teeming with million upon million of strange humpbacked cattle. "I found such a quantity of cows [bison]," Coronado reported, "that it is impossible to number them, for while I was journeying through these plains, until I returned to where I first found them, there was not a day that I lost sight of them." Following along after these apparently endless herds were parties of nomadic hunters— ancestral Lipan Apaches, or Quechero Indians—who dressed in bison-skin clothing (sewn with bison sinew, drawn through a bison-bone awl), slept in bison-hide tipis, and subsisted on a diet of bison blood and bison muscle. Even the grass in this new world was cause for amazement, as it rebounded from the conquistadors' steps and erased the trace of their presence. In this great round world, all that glittered was grass and an ecosystem of such richness and diversity that it could scarcely be credited.

But think how amazed Coronado would have been if he had somehow been able to sense the true extent and variety of North America's grasslands. Little did he know that he had set foot on a vast prairie heartland—a continent of grass—that was flanked on every side by smaller islands of grassland and prairie-to-forest transitions, or savannas. To the north, for instance, beyond his farthest imaginings, lay the Peace River Parklands, a region of rolling grass and poplars that marked the frontier between the Great Plains grasslands and the boreal forest. To the east, the Prairie-and-Oak Transition Zone— a tongue of prairie interspersed with groves of hardwoods— extended to the Great Lakes and beyond, marking the interface between the grasslands and the eastern deciduous forest. To the south, the prairies merged and melted into sultry, soupy marshlands to produce the semitropical vistas of the Western Gulf Coastal Grasslands. And to the west, in the broad valleys of the western Cordillera, lay the California Grasslands—spangled in spring by lupines and yellow-orange poppies—and the arid Palouse Grasslands of the Great Basin. Dominated by scraggly stands of sagebrush and spiky, sparse grasses, the Palouse, or bunchgrass, prairie stretched along the drainage of the Columbia and Snake Rivers to intergrade with the shrubby growth of the Montana Valley Grasslands.

And in the center of everything there was the main attraction, the Great Plains Grasslands themselves, a landscape that even today invites wonderment. This truly is big sky country, with horizons that extend from the boreal forests of Alberta, Saskatchewan, and Manitoba to the deserts of the American Southwest and from the foothills of the Rockies to the Mississippi drainage. The numbers speak for themselves. Length: 2,400 kilometers (1,500 miles). Width: between 600 and 1,100 kilometers (between 400 and 700 miles). Vaguely triangular in outline, the region is broadest toward the north and narrows to its apex in the Hill Country of central Texas. Total area: 2.6 million square kilometers (1 million square miles), or roughly 14 percent of the entire landmass of Canada, Alaska, and the Lower Forty-Eight states.

THEN AND NOW

It is one thing to send our minds running across the contours of the Great Plains grasslands. It is quite another to bring these spaces to life, to try to perceive them in their full, natural vitality and splendor. What would it have been like to step out onto the round bowl of the southern grasslands with Coronado in 1541, aware that at any moment our progress might be blocked by a dusty, pawing, milling herd of bison? Or, precisely 150 years later, in 1691, to have traveled with Henry Kelsey and his Cree and Assiniboine guides from Hudson Bay through the northern forest and onto the prairies of the Saskatchewan River country? What emotion would have seized us when a blocky, hunched shadow gradually resolved into the form of a massive and potentially lethal grizzly bear? Or what if we could slip back in time to 1804 (a mere two hundred years ago) and join Lewis and Clark on their famous expedition up the Missouri River?

Imagine: Bison beyond counting. ("I do not think I exaggerate," Lewis wrote as he crossed the Dakota plains in 1804, "when I estimate the number of Buffaloe which could be compre[hend]ed at one view to amount to 3000.") Flights of pronghorns at every turn. Elk coming up out of misty valleys to graze on the prairie at dawn. Bighorn sheep perched on the steep, crumbling walls of the Little Missouri badlands. Wolves threading across the prairies, trailing the herds.

Two hundred years isn't very long on the geologic time scales of planet Earth. These memories lie at the very threshold of the present, so close that we half expect to be able to walk into a fold in the landscape and encounter them. And something like this still occasionally happens when we stumble across a physical trace of the past, whether it's a flaked stone tool that once belonged to a bison hunter or a shallow, saucer-shaped hollow that was worn into the dirt by generations of rolling, grunting bison. The animals have vanished, but the imprint of their flesh and blood is still on the land. It is all so mind-bogglingly recent.

There are not many places where the wild is as close at hand as it is on the Great Plains. In the Old World of Europe and

Asia, no one can quite remember what "natural" looked like, because the land has been successively shaped and reshaped to meet human needs for hundreds or thousands of years. But in the New World of the prairies—right up to the moment when the settlement boom began—humans had lived off the natural productivity of this vast, sun-swept expanse of grass. From the time of their arrival on the plains, some eleven thousand years before, the First Peoples had drawn their sustenance from the native animals and plants, experiencing both feast and famine as hunters and gatherers. This is not to say that they sat back passively and let nature take its course. They were active participants in the ecosystem, ready and willing to use whatever technologies they could command to improve their chances of survival. For example, they had no qualms about setting the prairies on fire to green up the grass and draw bison in for the hunt. They tilled the soil of fertile river valleys and planted gardens of sunflowers, corn, and squash. They eagerly adapted to the new culture of firearms and horses.

Yet despite these human innovations, the underlying dynamic of the ecosystem—the interplay between climate and grasses, grazers and predators—remained robust. A landscape that had evolved to support large herds of grazing animals was still doing exactly that, as life ebbed and flowed in time with the seasons. Then, in the early to mid-1800s, the pace of change accelerated. In far-off Washington and Ottawa, ambitious governments began to assert their claim to the land and resources of the Great Plains. As a prelude to agricultural settlement, Native people were confined on reserves and reservations, whether by persuasion or by brute force, and the bison on which they depended—the multitudes of "humpbacked cattle" that had darkened the plains—were virtually wiped out in a bloody orgy of killing. Tellingly, the final stages of this slaughter were motivated by the discovery that bison hides could be cut and sewn into leather belts and used to power machines in the burgeoning industrial complex in the East. (The last free-roaming bison were killed in Canada in 1883 and in the U.S. in 1891.) Modern times had arrived on the prairies.

And then came the settlers, an onrush of humanity that reached full flood in the late 1800s and early 1900s. Determined to make a stand in this new country, the incomers quickly progressed from temporary shacks and shanties into substantial homes, making them the first people ever to establish permanent, year-round dwellings on the open plains. This was a bold experiment, occasioned with far more risk than anyone at the time seemed to recognize or, at least, was prepared to admit. But whatever the hazards, the way forward was clear. The object was to assert control over the ecosystem and redirect its natural vitality into the production of commodities that could be bought and sold on the world market. Beef, not bison. Wheat and corn instead of prairie wool.

The result of this revolution is the landscape that we see today, a colorful patchwork of fields and rangelands, where geese feed in the stubble, foxes hunt in farmyards, and meadowlarks sing their hearts out on fence posts. These are the prairies that our generation was born to, and they are beautiful in their own right.

Yet the more we love this place as it is, the more we feel the pain of what it so recently was. The wild prairie ecosystem is gone. And this tragedy is compounded by the realization that we don't even know exactly what it is that we have lost. "Civilization" and "progress" overran the grasslands with such an urgent rush that the ecosystem was disrupted before anyone had a chance to make a systematic study of exactly what was out there or to figure out how all the pieces interacted with each other. The people who might have had the most to teach us— the last generation of hunters and gatherers—went to their graves largely unheeded by the newcomers, taking their knowledge of the prairie and its lifeways with them. We are left with little to guide us except for fragments of written descriptions in the journals of explorers and early settlers—partial lists of species, brief sightings, and offhand remarks—that leave many basic questions unanswered.

The depth of our ignorance is startling. Question: How many bison were there on the plains before the slaughter began? Answer: No one can tell us with any assurance. By working and reworking the available strands of evidence, experts have estimated the precontact population at anywhere from 12 million to 125 million animals, a variance that leaves more than 100 million bison in limbo. Although the currently accepted figure sets the herds at some 30 million, no one really knows. And if we cannot account for big things like bison, how much less do we know about the smaller and less conspicuous organisms—little things like insects and spiders, fish and frogs, rodents and songbirds—that lived and died in their untold variety and interest and abundance? Yet if the wild past is lost to us, we can still look ahead. Despite everything that has happened, it is not too late to acknowledge the natural forces that continue to animate the prairie world and that, even today, shape the lives of all its creatures.

URBAN

COYOTES

The Trickster in Toronto

A cluster of people stands at the edge of a cottonwood grove, their faces raised to the evening sky. Eyes tight shut, lips pursed, they yip and howl like wild things, then wait. As the human ululation fades, a rising cry echoes back across the woods. Coyotes? Or the wailing of fire sirens? Hard to be sure when you're in the heart of one of North America's largest urban centers.

For the past decade, coyotes have been denning on the Leslie Street Spit, a finger of land extending into Lake Ontario about four kilometers (two and a half miles) from midtown Toronto. According to Scott Jarvie, coordinator of environmental projects for the Toronto and Region Conservation Authority (and leader of the coyote howl), the animals now occupy virtually every major park in and around the city. What's more, coyotes have taken up residence in many other cities across the continent, from Vancouver and Los Angeles to Halifax and New

York. Not bad for a species that two hundred years ago was at home only in the wide open spaces of the western grasslands. By 1995, when the first coyotes reached Prince Edward Island, the animals had laid claim to all but the northernmost regions of the continent.

The story of this remarkable expansion reads like an episode from the Native myth of Coyote the Trickster. For coyotes have prospered in the face of a determined human effort to stop them. Frustrated by depredations on livestock (especially calves and lambs), we have pursued them with every weapon at hand. When leghold traps and bullets failed us, we baited them with poison and set dynamite in their dens. Even today, an estimated 350,000 to 400,000 coyotes are killed every year in the United States alone, and in Canada, where no central registry is kept, the annual death toll must surely run to five or six figures.

Yet in the face of this persecution, the resourceful coyote has gotten the better of us by taking advantage of every opportunity that we chanced to offer. For example, by clearing forests for farming, we inadvertently opened up new coyote habitat; then by exterminating wolves, the coyotes' main natural predator, we removed the only force that might have limited their expansion. Even *killing* coyotes creates opportunities for the survivors, since it provides them with access to plentiful prey and den sites. These resources are quickly translated into litters of bright-eyed pups, which in turn rebuild and extend the population. One way or another, it seems, coyotes always triumph.

The Toronto coyotes are a case in point. Although the animals had established themselves around Lake Ontario by the early 1900s, they were pushed aside as Toronto expanded. Unable to survive in a landscape of pavement and postage-stamp-sized lawns—without enough small mammals to eat or seclusion for rearing their young—the coyotes retreated outside the city limits. At the time, most people probably thought that that was where they belonged. The city was for people, the country for animals. But attitudes have "greened" since then, and city dwellers now demand a touch of nature in their urban habitat. Over the past ten to fifteen years, green spaces have been expanded, parks have been "naturalized," and areas like the Leslie Street Spit have been allowed to go wild. Once these improvements were made, it wasn't long before coyotes moved in to take advantage of them.

For Jarvie, the return of Toronto's coyotes is a mark of success. "For many people, an urban park or a ravine provides a first exposure to the natural world. Predators, including coyotes, ought to be part of the picture. Most of the people I talk to are glad they are there, providing more balance to the local ecosystem."

But living next door to the Trickster, satisfying though it may be, can also be challenging. Ten years ago, Jarvie typically received one or two calls a year from residents who thought they had sighted wolves. But as the coyote population has grown, so has the number of calls. Jarvie now fields two to three dozen complaints a year, primarily during the breeding season (winter through spring), when coyotes are most vocal, most active, and most hungry. "There's a coyote in my compost." "A coyote bit my dog." "A coyote nipped at my shopping bag and followed me through High Park."

Although some callers demand action—they want the "problem" removed—Jarvie believes that the solution lies in public education. Even if it were feasible to slaughter coyotes in the city (which clearly it is not), coyote control has proved to be a universal failure. Relocating "nuisance animals" won't work either, because coyotes are notoriously difficult to catch; the Trickster is not about to walk into a live trap. Supposing a coyote could be removed, its place would quickly be filled, and the newcomer would doubtless find some way of getting into trouble.

If coyotes aren't about to change their ways, then humans will have to adapt. "We need to teach people how to prevent potential problems," says Jarvie. Since coyotes sometimes kill cats and small dogs, every pet should be kept on a leash—"right on your heel, not twenty feet ahead on an extendable lead." Even more important, coyotes should never be fed, either accidentally (by leaving garbage lying around) or on purpose (in an effort to help them). "Coyotes have moved into the city because there is good habitat for them here. They do not require supplementary food." Animals that receive handouts from people lose their inborn fear and may start coming a bit too close for comfort.

Although coyotes can be unnerving, they aren't very dangerous. An adult human can easily scare them away by yelling or throwing rocks; small children, on the other hand, should be carefully watched. In the 1980s, a toddler was killed by a coyote in Los Angeles, the only recorded instance of such a tragedy. (Fortunately, coyotes do not often become rabid.)

By crossing the final frontier into the city, coyotes have added their own wild note to the urban environment. With a few commonsense precautions, we can enjoy their proximity and even hope to live with them in natural harmony.

DANCES

WITH BISON

The Wild and the Tame

When fifty plains bison are thundering straight at you, you notice. The glint of horns, the blur of hooves, the onrush of power and mass. Suddenly, the thick wall of bales that has been provided as a shield for spectators looks worryingly delicate. These bison are only youngsters—a herd of yearlings from Elk Island National Park in Alberta that was moved here, to the wide open spaces of the Old Man on His Back Prairie and Heritage Conservation Area near Eastend, in southwestern Saskatchewan, at the end of 2003. Now, six months later, they are being pushed out of the small acclimation pasture where they spent the winter and into their new home, twelve hundred hectares (nearly three thousand acres) of rolling native grassland atop a high, windswept plateau.

Young as they are, these bison are heart-stoppingly big and fast. They drum straight toward the barrier and then, with seconds to spare, swing left, charge past the huddle of onlookers, and make a dash for the open range. Within minutes, they have slowed to a trot and a walk and settled down to graze. Their great heavy heads lowered to the grass, they flow out across the land, toward what appear to be untrammeled horizons. A whoop of elation goes up from the viewing stand.

In my mind's eye, I multiply those thrilling dark forms by a hundred, a thousand, a million, remembering the accounts I've read of the old days, when some 30 million bison coursed across the grasslands of half a continent, from the Canadian prairies south to Texas and from the Rocky Mountains east to the Mississippi drainage. In the early 1800s, for example, North West Company fur trader Alexander Henry wrote about traveling through herds so large that he could not estimate their extent, even after climbing up into a tree to get a better view of them. "The ground was covered [by bison] at every point of the compass, as far as the eye could reach," he noted of one such sighting, and as the herd traveled beneath him, the entire prairie for miles around seemed to be alive and moving.

By the 1880s, however, those millions had been blasted into oblivion by an influx of market hunters on the advancing front of "civilization." Only a few hundred stragglers survived the onslaught, most of them south of the Canada–U.S. line, to become the direct ancestors of all the bison now alive.

But before I can bring these lost worlds into focus, I am brought back to the present by the clatter of camera shutters and the whirring of power drives, as the journalists clustered behind the bales scurry to meet their deadlines. By nightfall, people across the country will have heard the good news that bison are roaming freely on the prairies for the first time in more than a hundred years. Many who hear it will no doubt believe that it's true.

It's not, of course. Not exactly. For just beyond the reach of the cameras lie the signs of a century of change: parked cars, stubble fields, disheveled farm buildings. Shiny new steel-wire fencing stretches across the hills, designed so that deer will jump over, pronghorns scoot under, and bison will stay in. Truth to tell, the bison at Old Man on His Back are confined in a pasture, albeit a largish one, and there is nothing particularly newsworthy about fenced-in bison. There are currently some 1,500 commercial bison producers on the prairies with a combined herd of around 150,000 animals, according to the Canadian Bison Association. So, what's so special about these 50 bison, compared to all the rest? And who should really take the kudos for reintroducing bison and preserving prairie grasslands for the great bovids to feed on? Is the rumble at Old Man on His Back nothing but hype and spin, or is there more to the story than will fit in a thirty-second news clip?

THE SAVE MENTALITY

When rancher Peter Butala took the steps that eventually led to the bison release, he was not thinking about attracting publicity. He just wanted to save his grass, the 5,300 hectares (13,000 acres) of native prairie on the Old Man on His Back plateau, where he had lived and ranched since childhood. That was back in the mid-1980s, at a time when the government—continuing the policy of plow-it-up-and-plant-it that had dominated the West since agricultural settlement began—was still paying ranchers to grub up their native pasture and plant it to tame forages. Like the bison before them, the natural grasslands were becoming a thing of the past. (Today, less than 19 percent of the original mixed-grass prairie in Saskatchewan remains intact and, though government policy has shifted slightly in favor of conservation, more is lost each year.) With eight hundred hectares (two thousand acres) of his own place under cultivation, Butala knew from experience that the tame forages would not prove out and that, after an initial burst of high production, the result would be disappointment. In his eyes, the lasting value of his land lay in the native grass, and he was determined to do whatever he could to protect it.

A tall, quiet man who gazes out at the world from under a Stetson, Butala is not given to flowery outbursts. "I just didn't want to see the prairie get broke up when I retired," he says. "I like to see the grass in good condition, fairly thick, headed out, not grazed too hard. I like to see it looking healthy."

It took ten years of trying before he and his wife, author Sharon Butala, found a like-minded partner in the Nature Conservancy of Canada, which acquired the property from them, through a combination of purchase and gift, in 1996. Since then the place has been operated by its new owners as a working ranch, with cattle—and now bison—on the land under careful, conservation-minded management. The goal is to use grazing as a tool to keep both the grasses and the grassland ecosystem in good health, not just now but, as the Nature Conservancy dares to promise, forever.

Over the years, the ranching industry has been deservedly criticized for its destructive impact on places like the Amazon rain forest and the desert grasslands of the United States, environments that are not naturally suited to livestock production. But the North American prairies are different. If ever there was a landscape that was made to be grazed, this is it, an ecosystem that evolved in the presence of bison and other grass-guzzlers by the millions. Through a long process of co-adaptation with grazers, prairie grasses have developed roots that are richly stocked with nutrients, for rapid regrowth, as well as nibble-proof growing points that are protected by the soil. If you chew a grass stem down to the quick, it will shoot right back up again, as if immune to discouragement. And as the grasses respond to the patchy, mouthful-by-mouthful influence of grazing, they grow up to create a patchy mosaic of habitats—from thick, waving stands for bobolinks, in places where little grazing has occurred, to stubby, chewed-off openings for horned larks and killdeer. Grazing is the engine that makes the prairie ecosystem work.

Although cattle can keep grasslands in decent shape, as a century of ranching has proved, they don't bring the same credentials to the job as bison do. Bison are built for the prairies, a four-legged expression of winter blizzards and summer droughts, with ten thousand years of evolution and experience to back them up. So when the opportunity arose to reintroduce a conservation herd of bison to part of the Old Man on His Back land, Butala—now semi-retired from ranching but still an active member of the project's advisory board—was solidly in support.

"I was brought up on the save mentality," he says. "You were always thinking ahead, always trying to have something in reserve for the future. It feels good to see the bison out there. It feels good to be doing this."

THE BISON ADVANTAGE

"I hope you haven't been talking to the people at the Nature Conservancy," snaps Dr. Marshall Patterson. A stalwart of the Canadian bison industry, Patterson is a veterinarian, a rancher, a long-time adviser to the Saskatchewan Bison Association, and a past president of the national organization of commercial bison producers. "We [bison producers] have been having a bit of a running gunfight with them about their alleged wild herd down at Old Man on His Back," he says. "They make it sound like it's the only pure bison herd in the country, somehow better than domestically raised bison, and on and on. From our perspective, they haven't portrayed it honestly at all."

Patterson and bison go back a long way. In the late 1980s, at the same time that the Butalas were working to save their land, he found himself in Regina, as the agricultural diversification specialist for the province, working to save the whole enterprise of livestock production. With the economy reeling from the double hit of a record-breaking drought and disastrous grain prices, he assessed the available options and came up with one that seemed to hold promise. The best way forward for agriculture, he became convinced, was to bring back the bison.

Bison ranching had taken place on a small scale ever since agricultural settlement began, but it had never acquired the gravitas of beef production. Yet as Patterson and others began to point out in the late 1980s and early 1990s, there was good reason for producers to cash in on the "bison advantage." On the debit side of the ledger, costs would be lower than they were for cattle, because bison were adapted to the prairies and could generally fend for themselves. On the credit side, bison produced a low-fat, low-cholesterol meat that was likely to fetch a premium price in an increasingly health-conscious market.

And if the arithmetic looked favorable for producers, the domestication of bison also held out benefits for the environment. Not only would native grasslands be conserved as pasture, but marginal cropland (land that should never have been plowed up in the first place) would be seeded to tame hay, thereby preventing exposed soil from blowing away. What's more, a once-dominant species, long absent from the scene, would be restored to its rightful place on the prairie.

Sure enough, ten to fifteen years later, herds of domesticated bison now graze peacefully in farmers' fields from one end of the Great Plains to the other. Although the bison market is currently in the dumps—there have been problems with over-supply, insufficient slaughter facilities, and the closure of the Canada–U.S. border due to BSE (bovine spongiform encephalopathy)—expectations remain buoyant. And Patterson is candidly proud of the part that he and his industry have played in domesticating bison and making a place for them in the modern agricultural environment. In his view, plains bison are being conserved by the bison industry, without any help from "the Nature Conservancy types."

BISON FOLLIES

If someone were to show you two plains bison, one from a domestic herd and the other from Old Man on His Back, you would not likely be able to tell which was which. By contrast, if one of the animals were a wood bison—a bigger, burlier subspecies from the forests of northern Alberta and the Northwest Territories—the differences would be easier to detect, but that's another story. Plains bison look very similar wherever you find them, whether they are being managed commercially or for conservation. Yet there's more to a bison than meets the eye, and even near look-alikes may harbor hidden differences in genetics. Over the last decade, scientists have discovered that many (probably most) of the plains bison alive today carry cattle DNA, the result of an early and, for the most part, abandoned enthusiasm for cross-breeding. Although nobody knows what effect, if any, the foreign genes may have, these animals are clearly not purebreds but cattle-bison hybrids. The only known exceptions in Canada are the plains bison at Elk Island National Park and their direct descendants, including the animals at Old Man on His Back. And thereby hangs a tangled tale of chance and mischance.

The ancestors of the Elk Island herd arrived there in 1906, but their saga really began thirty years earlier. In 1872, a year when 2 million bison were killed for their hides—their carcasses left to rot—a Pend d'Orielle man named Samuel Walking Coyote took the exceptional step of gathering seven orphaned calves and leading them from the Milk River country of Alberta to his home on the Flathead Reservation in western Montana. The story goes that he had acquired a second wife on his travels and was bringing the bison home as a gesture of mollification. These animals soon passed into the hands of local ranchers Charles Allard and Michel Pablo, the latter a re-formed buffalo hunter who wanted to make amends for his part in the slaughter. For several decades thereafter, Pablo and Allard profited from these zoological rarities, selling hides and mounted heads and supplying live animals to parks, zoos, and other ranches. But when the Flathead lands were appropriated for homesteading in the early 1900s, the open range came to an end and the herd—now the largest in existence, at more than seven hundred head—was put on the market.

At first, it looked as if the bison would be purchased by the U.S. government, but a tight-fisted Congress stymied that idea. Meanwhile, news of the opportunity sped north to Banff, Alberta, where it reached the ear of park superintendent Howard Douglas. A committed conservationist who already oversaw a small herd of bison in Rocky Mountain (now Banff) National Park, Douglas persuaded his superiors to buy the Pablo-Allard outfit and transport the animals to Elk Island. After a brief stopover there, the herd would then be moved again to their real home, a brand-new Buffalo National Park near Wainwright, Alberta.

In the event, however, about fifty of the animals at Elk Island evaded capture and had to be left behind. The rest of the herd were duly transported to southern Alberta, where some of them were used by the Department of Agriculture for its cross-breeding work. In the 1920s, thousands of surplus animals from the Wainwright herd, by now genetically suspect and infected with cattle diseases such as brucellosis and tuberculosis, were shipped north to the Wood Buffalo National Park, thereby compromising the future of the only surviving population of wood bison. By 1940, the park at Wainwright had been disbanded, the bison dispersed, and the land transferred to the armed forces.

The remnant herd at Elk Island, however, has been spared these tribulations. By the dumbest of dumb luck, they still breed true to their ancestral stock, making them one of only nine known source populations of 100-percent-pure-and-unadulterated bison anywhere in the world, and the only one in Canada. The others are all in parks and wildlife refuges in the United States. Better yet, the scientists tell us that the Elk Island herd is also genetically rich, with little sign of deterioration due to inbreeding. If we want to conserve the Real Thing, this is it.

WILD PROSPECTS

The population of bison in western Canada has rebounded more than one hundred thousandfold in just over a hundred years, from the killing fields of the 1870s to the carefully managed pastures of the present. Although nowhere near their historic abundance, bison are no longer painfully rare. Yet in the face of this apparent recovery, the Committee on the Status of Endangered Wildlife in Canada has recently recommended that plains bison be listed as a threatened species under the Species at Risk Act. If this recommendation is accepted by Cabinet as anticipated, plains bison will become a national conservation priority for the first time ever.

"Ninety-seven percent of the bison alive today are in the commercial herd," says University of Calgary professor Cormack Gates, co-chair of the National Bison Recovery Team and North American chair of the Bison Specialist Group of the World Conservation Union. "When it comes to conservation, domesticated livestock just don't have what it takes."

For one thing, there's the question of genetic mixing, which is known to be widespread in the commercial herd. "Animals that carry cattle genes are not wild-type bison," Gates points out. "They have been altered for human purposes."

And therein lies a deeper problem. The goal of livestock production, whether it's achieved or not, is to create a product that can be sold at a profit. With this bottom line in mind, the animals are bred selectively to bring out traits that make them fit not for survival in the wild but for commercial purposes. So even leaving aside the question of genetic purity, the domestic herd cannot contribute to conservation, Gates contends, because it is being shaped by human needs rather than by natural forces.

"We can breed bison for docility," Gates says, "and this is being done. We can shorten their legs, broaden their backs for meat production. We can do all of this. The real question is: Can we conserve the original plains bison?"

Whatever the benefits of ranching to conservation—and they are considerable and real, particularly in conserving grasslands—the livestock industry is not in the business of maintaining threatened species. As evidence, Gates points to the fate of the aurochs, *Bos primigenius*, the wild Eurasian ungulate from which most modern breeds of cattle are descended. "The last aurochs died in a zoo in 1627," he says, "and all the diverse genetic material in that gene pool was lost. It would be miserable to do the same thing to plains bison."

Whether or not that happens depends, in Canada, solely on the purebred bison in the source population at Elk Island and their descendants—around 1,000 animals in five small herds—that are being managed for conservation. This number includes the 250 to 270 animals at Elk Island, the 50 at Old Man on His Back, and another 700 in three genuinely wild and free-ranging herds: one at Pink Mountain in northern British Columbia, one on the Primrose Lake Air Weapons Range in northeastern Alberta, and one on the southwestern boundary of Prince Albert National Park in central Saskatchewan. Overall, these populations are increasing and, with no impediment in their way, are expected to continue to do so for the foreseeable future. The cause of wild survival will get a big boost during the winter and spring of 2005 and 2006, when a shipment of calves from Elk Island is scheduled to be delivered to the west block of Grasslands National Park, in south-central Saskatchewan, and turned loose on 21,000 hectares (50,000 acres) of native grassland in the spectacular Frenchman River valley. Similar projects are also being considered for Waterton Lakes and Banff National Parks.

Far off on the conservation horizon lies the dream of creating a much larger refuge to which plains bison—and perhaps wolves and grizzlies—could one day be restored, under a scheme that would connect the Old Man on His Back property and Grasslands National Park in Saskatchewan with the

Charles M. Russell Wildlife Refuge in Montana. "This is a very long-range vision," Gates stresses, "and it could only happen if the local ranching community were in full support. Perhaps it will never be feasible, but it is nice to imagine." If this dream does one day come true, it will be a tribute to people who, like the Butalas, are devoted to the "save mentality" that is so much a part of life in next-year country. By conserving the true plains bison, we open up the chance that the Wild West lies out ahead of us and not just in the past.

A FUTURE
FOR GRIZZLIES

Artemis Beckons

"*T*he reason that grizzlies are not extinct is that they have power." George Blondin is known among the Dene of the Northwest Territories as an elder, a term that honors wisdom as well as age. A robust man in his sixties, he sits at a plain desk in a bare-walled basement office. Outside the high window are rows of parked cars and the snow-hushed bustle of northern city life. But George Blondin is not of the city, and as he talks, his mind travels the land and rivers near Great Bear Lake, the country of his youth.

"I mean mental power. Bears use it to turn people away, to keep hunters from killing them in their dens. Otherwise, they would all have been shot."

There was the time, he recalls, when a visitor (not an Indian) went on a winter bear hunt with a Dene father and son. When they found a grizzly in a den, the visitor brashly predicted that they would all be eating bear the next day. The Dene warned him not to be crude. You can't talk bluntly about "eating bear"; you must use terms of respect. But the visitor went on prattling.

Next morning, when he and the hunters went back to claim their prize, the father and son took turns poking a stick in the den to rouse the dormant bear. They stood back, tense, waiting for the animal to emerge. Nothing happened. Again they prodded. Still nothing. Finally, one after the other, they crawled gingerly into the cavity. The grizzly was not there; it had taken offense and disappeared.

Blondin offers this story as proof that bears have powers of understanding. They are the only animals, he says, who can read our thoughts and understand human speech.

He remembers that his father spoke to every bear he met. "Grandfather," he would say, "we don't mean you any harm. Please don't hurt us. Let us go our way and bring us luck on our hunt." The grizzly, hearing these calm words and honorable intentions, would turn and walk away. "If you speak from the heart," Blondin maintains, "bears will understand." He knows; he is speaking from experience.

Among all these wonders, what impresses him most about grizzlies is their ability to hibernate. Each fall, when the roots and berries on which they rely for food wither in the cold, grizzly bears dig dens in the ground, curl up inside, and wait for winter to pass. For as long as seven months, they do not eat, drink, or pass wastes. When they emerge in the spring, they return again to regular life, as if they have been reborn. Some of the females come out of their dens with tiny cubs, born while the mothers slept. Birth and rebirth in one.

"It's amazing," Blondin says, shaking his head. "How can any animal do that?"

One theory, which he remembers from the elders of his youth, is that hibernating bears nourish themselves by sucking fat through their paws. This is an odd idea and at first hearing may seem of no great significance. But to encounter it here, in a drab office, in the last decade of the twentieth century, is a jolt. Anthropologists think that this idea is well over ten thousand years old. By its very oddity, this homely scrap of folklore serves as a "tag" that helps identify a rich complex of practices and beliefs that spans three continents and more than a hundred centuries.

THE BEAR GODDESS

The vision of the grizzly that George Blondin articulates was once common across Eurasia and North America, from Scandinavia to Japan, over the Bering Strait, south to the Columbia River, and east to Labrador. Until very recently, bear rites, some simple, some complex, were practiced by many of the traditional peoples of the Northern Hemisphere: the Saamis (Lapps), Finns, Ostyak, Olcha, Vogul, Gilyak, Ainu, Tsimshian, Haida, Tlingit, Sahtu Dene, Cree, Ojibwa, Mi'kmaq, Delaware, and others. Although no two of these cults were exactly alike, they were linked by similar beliefs, customs, and purposes. Scholars believe that these cults originated among ancient Asian hunters, whose descendants brought them to North America at the end of the Ice Age, or earlier still, among the ancient people who honored cave bears.

As Swedish anthropologist Carl-Martin Edsman points out, "Remarkable finds of ritually buried bear skulls and bones in stone-age caves in the Alpine region and the South of France present great resemblances with rites still observed among the northern hunting peoples, and thus testify to the age of these ceremonies and the conceptions corresponding to them."

In its time, the cave bear, *Ursus spelaeus,* was the most bearish of bears, ferocious and huge, and may have been hunted and honored by humankind for forty thousand years. But when it became extinct, about ten thousand years ago, the veneration passed to other bears, especially the grizzly, *Ursus arctos horribilis*. The most widely distributed species of bear in the world, the grizzly—or brown bear, as it is also known—spans the world of the bear ceremonies. (*Ursus arctos horribilis* is known by different names in different parts of the world. In Europe and areas of Alaska, the species is known as the brown bear, but in the rest of North America, it is called the grizzly. Other terms, such as *higuma,* red bear, and horse bear, are used in Japan, India, and Tibet. To avoid the awkwardness of composite names, such as grizzly/brown bear, the word *grizzly* is used here in an expanded sense to refer to all races of *Ursus arctos horribilis,* wherever they occur.)

At the heart of the ceremonies, scholars say, there lies a myth, perhaps inspired by grizzlies and certainly of great antiquity. We glimpse it in figurines made in Yugoslavia and Greece during the New Stone Age, seven thousand years ago—miniature terra-cotta statues of a goddess with the head of a bear, nursing a bear cub. It is echoed in Slavic birth customs that identify a new mother as "the bear" and in the festival of Panagia Arkoudiotissa, "Virgin Mary of the Bear," which is celebrated on the second day of February at a cave in western Crete. We remember it clearly in stories that are still sometimes told in Sweden, Finland, Siberia, and Canada. Of these, the version from the British Columbia coast, as recorded by anthropologist Marius Barbeau in the *Journal of American Folklore,* is the best known.

It seems that long ago, there was a young girl named Peesunt who often went into the mountains with her friends to pick huckleberries. But instead of singing to warn the bears of her presence, as she should have done, she chatted and laughed disrespectfully. One day, when she and her friends were returning home with heavy baskets of fruit, Peesunt's pack strap broke and she was left behind. Evening fell, and out of the darkness came two young men, "looking like brothers," who offered to help.

As she followed them up the mountain, Peesunt noticed that they were wearing bear robes. They led her to their home where several other people, dressed in the same way, sat around a fire. "The white mouse Tseets—Grandmother—came to her and pulled at her robe, which was now coated with long grey hair like a bear's. And the mouse squeaked, 'Granddaughter, the bears have taken you to their den; from now on you shall be one of them, bearing children.'" Peesunt became the wife of one of the spirit bears and bore twins, who were half human and half grizzly.

All this time, Peesunt's human brothers were searching for her. Eventually, they located her, climbed up to the den, and killed her bear husband. Before he died, the bear taught his wife two ritual songs, "which the hunters should use over his dead body," to ensure good fortune. Peesunt's sons became expert bear hunters, and through their help and the protection of the dirge songs, she and her people prospered.

Peesunt is the Bear Mother, the "sacred virgin" of the Saamis, who overcomes the division between human and animal, matter and spirit, profane and divine. Through her, the people receive the skills and ritual knowledge they need to ensure that grizzlies and other animals will come back to them and permit themselves to be hunted. By honoring the grizzly bear as they have been taught, the people will survive.

In Swedish, courtship or betrothal is still sometimes spoken of as "bear-capture," in distant remembrance, perhaps, of the Bear Mother and of a time when each new human family reenacted the sacred compact of the mythic bear marriage. We allude to the bear too in our words for motherhood, through the Old European root *bher* and the Germanic *beran,* which means "to bear children," the Germanic *barnum* ("bairn," or "child"), and the Old Norse *burdh* ("birth").

Among the Ainu, the aboriginal people of northern Japan, women sometimes acted on these associations by nursing and rearing young bears. In their culture, well into the twentieth century, this was the first step of preparation for an elaborate ceremony called *Iyomante,* or "sending home," in which grizzly bears were honored as intermediaries with their god. (The grizzly is "frightening, unpredictable, gentle, intelligent, awe-inspiring, dangerous, and beautiful—like God," Canadian writer Sid Marty says, echoing the Ainu insight. "Maybe it is God, or one expression of Him.")

As part of the ritual, the captive cub was killed, for the Ainu observed that the god must die in order to be reborn. Later the bear's flesh was shared as a feast by members of the community. In their book *The Sacred Paw: The Bear in Nature, Myth and Literature,* Paul Shepard and Barry Sanders identify this as a form of sacrament: "To be joined with the god was experienced first—and continues to be most deeply felt—in the eating of the sacred body."

Wherever they are found in the Northern Hemisphere, bear ceremonies acknowledge and invoke the deep, contrasting emotions that grizzlies arouse. They speak of kinship and cordiality, for the slain bear is welcomed as an honored guest. They speak of fear, for even in death, the grizzly's anger must be deflected or atoned. They speak of respect, for when the bear's body has been ceremonially consumed, its bones are often buried with care and reverence. In this way, it is believed, the grizzly bear will be reborn and come to the hunters again.

The bear will be reborn—as it is reborn each spring from its den, as nature is reborn from the cold of winter, as humans may hope for rebirth from the cold of death.

SKY BEARS

The grizzly stands at the center of the spiral of life. People "have always suspected that certain animals are masters and keepers of important secrets," Paul Shepard says; the bear guards the secret of renewal. Overhead by night, the celestial bears write their cyclic message across northern skies. Two clusters of bright stars dominate the heavens in the Northern Hemisphere. Sometimes identified as the Big and Little Dippers, they are known in classical mythology as the Great Bear, Ursa Major, and the Little Bear, Ursa Minor. As the story is usually told, the Great Bear is identified with the nymph Callisto, who was turned into a bear as a punishment for committing adultery with Zeus. The Little Bear is her son, Arkas, the founding hero of Arkadia, the wild, mountainous interior of the Peloponnese. But it seems unlikely that the tale has come to us in its original form. Callisto, after all, is a woman-in-the-form-of-a-bear who, like the Bear Mother, made love with a god and, through her son, secured the future of her race. Her name is an epithet of Artemis, the bear goddess, in whose honor Athenian girls once masked themselves and danced as bears. Surely, her position in the heavens is an honorary one, and not a sign of disgrace.

The Greeks were not the only group to position the bear at the center of the night. To the Iroquois and the Mi'kmaq, some of these same stars revealed a bear pursued by seven hunters, whereas the Hindus counted out seven bears. In these traditions and others, the bear stars hold the center of the whirling firmament. The polestar, the hub around which the heavens turn, is the end of the Little Bear's tail, and the Great Bear, close by, offers sighting lines by which it can be found. To this day, we use it to get our "bearings" when we are lost.

Night by night, the heavenly bears draw the stars behind them, ushering in each new day. According to Hindu mythology, they are the whirlwind at the heart of the universe, the force that turns the life-giving wheel of the year. "The Great Bear is the ever-turning mandala in the sky," Shepard and Sanders say, and "the Pole Star... provides more than mere navigational guidance—serving as the still center of the wheel, offering spiritual bearings for the religious wanderer."

LONGING AND FEAR

Grizzly bears have meaning for people; they burn bright in the human mind. Even today, alienated as we are from the natural world, we can sense their power. A few decades ago, when roadside feeding of bears was permitted in several North American parks, people poured in by the thousands. Many of them were deliriously unwary—offering food from bare fingers and lifting their children onto the animals' backs. In a way that defies reason, we trust bears and want to be close to them.

Similar yearnings may help account for the phenomenal success of the teddy bear. Why should it be that we entrust our children to the comfort of toy bears? Across Europe and North America, millions of one-eyed, threadbare teddies (or Paddingtons or Poohs) work their magic every night. The teddy bear, or Teddy's bear, as it was originally called, was created in 1902 by a media event. In November of that year, U.S. president

Theodore Roosevelt went to Mississippi to help settle a boundary dispute. As a break from the negotiations, he went out hunting but had no success. So someone produced a bedraggled little bear cub on a lead and suggested that Roosevelt might like to shoot it. Roosevelt, to his credit, declined. "I draw the line," he said. "If I shot that little fellow, I couldn't look my own boys in the face again." A cartoonist with the *Washington Post* used the event to satire the political negotiations, during which Roosevelt had also "drawn the line" at using his presidential powers to settle the dispute.

This image—the tough Rough Rider standing beside the spared cub—was widely publicized. Its political overtones were quickly forgotten, but the little bear was an instant success. The lovable, huggable bear-cub toy was put on the market in North America and Europe the following year, where it exerted a prompt and enduring appeal on adults and children alike. In twentieth-century culture, the teddy has virtually achieved the status of talisman, a protector against disorder and things that go bump in the night.

But our conception of the grizzly also has a darker side—a nightmare bear with glinting fangs and fiery eyes. Like our trust of bears, our terror is often extravagant. Grizzlies do kill people; that is beyond dispute. But such events are surprisingly rare. In North America, for example, visitors to mountain parks are more likely to be struck by lightning than to be killed by a grizzly bear. Yet when two campers were killed by grizzlies in Glacier National Park, the tragedy was distended into the plot of a horror film: "Eighteen feet of gut-crunching, man-eating terror!" the marquees trumpeted.

Our ancestors exploited similar feelings, and even the ancient bear ceremonies were not free of cruelty. The Ainu, for example, goaded their sacrificial bear with arrows before strangling it. The Romans, for their part, enrolled bears as gladiators in public spectacles. In AD 237, one thousand grizzlies are said to have been slaughtered in a single day. When the local supply of bears was exterminated, the emperors sent to North Africa for fighting stock, perhaps contributing to the eventual extinction of the African grizzly as well.

By the Middle Ages, such bloody entertainments had evolved into bearbaiting, a sport that remained popular in Europe for several centuries. In a typical bout, the grizzly was beaten, blinded, and tied to a post in the center of a bearbaiting pit. Dogs and men with whips were then turned loose upon it, and onlookers hooted and cheered as it tried to defend itself. Sometimes, for the further edification of the crowd, the bear was identified with the devil or a deadly sin, to be vanquished by a determined assault.

On the American frontier, such superficial allegories were not found necessary. Unabashed prize fights between grizzlies and Spanish bulls were enjoyed by Californians through most of the nineteenth century. Sometimes the bears, careless of their reputation for ferocity, refused to fight until they were goaded with nails on the ends of sticks, but usually they stood their ground and met their opponents head on. Strength met strength: the grizzly slashed with tooth and claw; the bull tore flesh with its sharp horns; and one or the other of the animals was eventually killed. These vicious spectacles were no doubt deeply satisfying to the frontiersmen because they proved that taming the wilderness was a godly and essential task. Who would wish to share their land with such gruesome beasts? The California grizzly was extinct by 1922.

Tragically, it is this negative image of the grizzly that has largely prevailed in the last few centuries. Under its persuasion, grizzlies have been knifed, harpooned, trapped, and poisoned. They have been lassoed by teams of horsemen and literally pulled apart; they have been set upon by dogs. Above all, they have been shot by the thousands or, more likely, by the hundreds of thousands. As British philosopher Thomas Carlyle once observed, the "genuine use" of gunpowder is to make "all men alike tall"; and high-powered guns have more than leveled the disparities between ourselves and bears. But rifles have not been our only weaponry. Bulldozers, chain saws, plows, and paving machines have all supported the attack.

Grizzly bears, clearly creatures with exceptional power to move the human mind, have been pushed slowly but relentlessly into a severe population decline. Two or three centuries ago, for example, there were about fifty thousand grizzlies in the contiguous United States; today there are fewer than fifteen hundred, occupying 1 percent of their former range. During the last century, the species has been exterminated in fourteen states and is now listed as "threatened" in the contiguous states.

In western Europe, the situation is equally precarious. In Sweden and Norway, once home to flourishing populations, there are now about 700 bears, and neighboring Finland has another 400 or 500. In Italy—miraculously—there are perhaps 65, mostly in Abruzzi National Park in the Apennines near Rome. Perhaps 120 remain in Spain; in France, no more than 30. A decade ago, the French population had ceased breeding and, had it not been for the introduction of animals from Slovenia, they would almost certainly have been lost. People had begun to speak of them as "walking dead."

In eastern Europe—especially the Carpathian and Balkan mountains—there are thought to be a few thousand bears. But in the Middle East and along the southern fringe of the species' range in Asia, extinction seems imminent. In Japan, the holy bears of the Ainu are now suffering what one biologist calls "horrendous persecution" in the interests of agriculture, forestry, and sport hunting.

All told, there are probably about 180,000 grizzlies in the world today. By far the majority—about 120,000—live in Russia. Sizable populations also inhabit Alaska (perhaps 30,000) and western Canada, mostly Yukon and British Columbia (another 20,000 or so). But as a Russian biologist has recently pointed out, even relatively large numbers offer "no basis for an attitude of calm." Alaskan researchers echo this anxiety: "Grizzlies are still abundant [in this state], fishing the same streams and traveling the same age-old trails as their ancestors did thousands of years ago. But many of the . . . pressures that led to the species' disappearance elsewhere are becoming evident in Alaska."

Around the hemisphere, those pressures are the same: loss of habitat and excessive shooting.

If we permit this process to continue, it will surely be a sign that we have lost our way. Guided by streetlights rather than starlight, we risk losing our connections with the forces that sustain and renew life on our planet. "The reason grizzlies are not extinct is that they have power," George Blondin says. Perhaps they will now have the power to help us change our way of life.

A QUESTION OF SURVIVAL

Grizzly bears need space, and the consensus is growing that large landscapes must be reserved for them if we wish to ensure that the species will survive—whole, healthy systems that still support wild populations of bears. Do it now, the experts urge, while we still have the chance. These areas won't have to be forbidden zones, where no human dare set foot. Grizzlies do not require untouched wilderness (if they did, there would be far fewer left). But they do need places where their interests are given top priority.

There are two main reasons for this need. First, most human activities reduce the quality of bear habitat. They leave the bears with less to eat and fewer places to sleep, mate, and den. Logging, for example, may remove brushy cover that the bears need for resting and safety, or destroy juicy underbrush that provides important food. In some ecosystems, logging also changes the character of the woodlands. Gone are the thickets, brambles, and berry bushes; in their place stand plantations with an empty forest floor. No place for a grizzly bear.

Other industries, agriculture, and recreation also take their toll. On rangelands, livestock compete with bears by trampling wetland plants and eating spring grass. Even something as benign as a hiking trail, which scarcely alters the land, may still reduce bear habitat. Most grizzlies avoid people, and if the human intrusion goes above some mysterious threshold (which varies from bear to bear), they may stop using areas that are otherwise rich and appealing.

Fortunately, grizzlies and people are both adaptable. Faced with a loss of resources, bears may be able to compensate in other parts of their range, or they may adapt to their reduced "standard of living" by producing fewer young. Faced with the prospect of losing bears, many people—loggers, ranchers, park managers, and others—have adjusted the way they do things to minimize the effect. With great care, and up to a point, humans and grizzlies can share the resources of the land.

So why the urgent need for protected areas? Added to the pressures on bear habitat is another, even more critical stress. For good reasons and bad, human beings shoot bears. The more people who use an area, the more bears are killed. "Grizzlies die of lead poisoning," says Stephen Herrero, chair and research supervisor of the Eastern Slope Grizzly Bear Project and former chair of the IUCN/Species Survival Commission Bear Specialist Group. "It's as simple as that."

One of North America's most productive populations of grizzlies lives in the Flathead Valley of southeastern British Columbia. Until a decade or so ago, this wild and rugged landscape remained largely untouched; then in rumbled the logging trucks. Close behind them came bear biologist Bruce McLellan, with a full kit of snares, tranquilizing darts, and radio collars, to find out how the bears would respond to development. "We didn't tell timber companies how to log," he recalls. "They just did it the way they were used to." A decade and more later, to his surprise and delight, the grizzly population was still in good health. "We found more bears there than anyone thought possible." In fact, McLellan thinks the bears may be poised for an upsurge.

But he is frankly worried about what the future will bring. The Flathead Valley is now easily accessible to anyone who cares to drive a logging road. They come in to hike, sketch, camp, or fish; it seems so innocent—and then somebody bumps into a grizzly in a berry patch or slops food around his or her campsite or blunders between a mother and her cub. A hunter leaves a carcass overnight and returns to find a snarling bear on top of it. People get annoyed or frightened or hurt, and grizzlies end up being shot.

And what if logging turns out to be the first step in a continuous process of development? Cabins, motels, ranches, mines—who knows what the future will bring? In other parts of British Columbia, forestry officials are suggesting that clearings created by logging should be used to pasture sheep. For grizzlies, the outcome would have the well-rehearsed inevitability of a nursery rhyme: "Bears kill people's sheep; sheep's people kill bears." In short order, the local grizzlies would be all but extinct, as they are on grazing lands elsewhere.

Farther north, Alaskan biologist John Schoen expresses similar concerns. Parts of his study area in southeastern Alaska have been logged in recent years. Here, he thinks, logging itself puts significant pressure on the bears, which stop using patches of forest that have been cut. But what concerns him far more is the number of bears that are now being killed. In one year, 20 percent of the local population was shot, far more than ever before. The reason: new roads and an unprecedented influx of humans.

It is a rule of thumb in bear management that no more than 5 or 6 percent of grizzlies in a given area should be killed by people each year. Most of these should be males. (After all, one male can breed with several females, and "surplus" males repress the population by killing cubs. Removing *some* of the males may actually permit the population to grow.) Stay within the guidelines, and the population will likely remain stable. Overstep them, and the bears will start to decline.

But how many grizzlies are there in the area? Five or 6 percent of what? This no one can say with certainty. Population figures are based on guesswork—elegant, educated guesswork, but guesswork nonetheless. Grizzly research is difficult, dangerous, and above all costly, with the result that few populations have been studied thoroughly. Managers must constantly extrapolate, using the little that is known to cast a dim, flickering light over vast areas of uncertainty. With the best intentions in the world, the process can go wrong, hunting limits may be set too high, and too many bears are shot.

This is not to say that hunters are the Bad Guys, or that no hunting should be allowed. Indeed, in several parts of the world, including France, Yugoslavia, Yukon, and the Northwest Territories, groups of hunters have taken the lead in bear conservation and research. It can also be argued that a carefully controlled, legal hunt is in the long-term interest of the bears, since it gives them the economic and political status of a "resource." Still, the whole undertaking is dicey.

The risks associated with hunting are compounded by other losses. Every year grizzlies are also killed as threats to human life or property. Often the action in these sorry incidents centers on trash. Garbage, particularly food waste, is a power-packed nutritional resource that no grizzly can ignore. Eleven years after the garbage dump was closed in Yellowstone National Park, grizzlies still nosed around the site, apparently hoping for one more bite. But as the Yellowstone experience proved, grizzlies that eat garbage often lose their fear of people, become dangerous, and get shot.

Such losses can often be prevented through proper garbage disposal, either by using incinerators or by transporting garbage to dumps outside of bear country—all garbage, every day, with no exceptions allowed. Back-country campers have a special responsibility to hang their garbage out of reach and keep their tent sites clean.

When these precautions are taken—as increasingly they are, by individuals, parks, towns, and industry—fewer grizzlies die. But given the nature of both people and bears, confrontations still arise, if not at the dump, then in the campground, the pasture, the orchard, or the bee yard. Sometimes problems can be resolved by airlifting "offending" grizzlies onto more remote terrain, though bears have a frustrating ten-

dency to come back home or get into mischief in their new lo-
cale. If the trouble is allowed to continue, female bears pass on
bad habits to the next generation, and human feelings may
eventually become so inflamed that they erupt in vengeance
and rage. In the long run, it may be better to accept the inevitable and shoot individual grizzlies that are known to pose
persistent threats.

To be realistic, we must also resign ourselves to an ongoing,
annual tally of "vandal kills." Grizzlies are shot illegally by mis-
trustful ranchers and by ignorant thrill seekers; how many animals are lost to these hooligans is not known, though the
number is thought to be significant. Tragically, there is no
doubt about the toll exacted by international criminal rings
that "harvest" bear body parts for an unsavory black-market
trade. As recently as 1997, for example, 6,061 bear gallbladders
were smuggled into Japan from Canada for use in traditional
medicine, where they fetched the tidy sum of U.S.$51,000.
Meanwhile, the price of a bowl of bear-paw soup, an Asian delicacy, has risen to U.S.$1,400 in the classy restaurants of China
and South Korea. Since the trade in bear paws is centered in
Asia, it threatens not only grizzlies but also the little-known
sloth, sun, and Asian black bears. "The fate of many of the
world's bear species will be decided in the next ten or twenty
years," warns grizzly expert Christopher Servheen of the University of Montana. By fate, he means survival.

A FUTURE FOR BEARS

Over the last several decades, much has been done to make
parts of the world safer for grizzly bears, through law enforce-
ment, public education, and management of human activities.
We have even begun, in a preliminary but practical way, to

acknowledge the hard economic realities of "limits to growth." By recycling, carpooling, and resisting the enticements of the latest "necessity," we may slow our incursion into grizzly range. But the future of the grizzly bear is still not assured. The margins of error are very small, yet we are certain to go on making mistakes, both technically and politically. It is with all this in mind that people who care about bears have begun to call for grizzly reserves.

Establishing these areas would not be a miracle cure. To ensure the future of the grizzly, we must continue to do everything we know how, everywhere that is practical, to the best of our ability. But if our best attempts go wrong (as history suggests they may), reserves would serve as a guarantee against total loss.

In British Columbia, the prime candidate for preservation is a misty coastal valley north of Prince Rupert called the Khutzeymateen. Here, in one of the last pristine watersheds on the West Coast, grizzlies forage in the lush undergrowth of an ancient rain forest. Overhead, bald eagles perch on Sitka spruce that began life in the twelfth century. Four species of salmon swim up the river to spawn. "There's everything a bear could want," says biologist and preservation advocate Wayne McCrory, who has conducted research in the area.

There's also everything a logger could want, and the future of the valley is in limbo, pending the results of a government study into the potential impact of logging on the bears and their habitat. In a province where cabinet ministers sometimes speak of woodlands as "fiber farms," the outcome is not guaranteed. If the Khutzeymateen were reserved, it would become Canada's first grizzly bear sanctuary and might serve as "core habitat" for a population of bears that could be safely maintained through the centuries. Similar proposals have been advanced elsewhere in western Canada and in Alaska, where several reserves have already been established.

These reserves would do much more than benefit grizzly bears. They would also create islands of wilderness, special places where the endless eccentric inventiveness of life could be studied, celebrated, and conserved. Lichens, voles, berry bushes, salamanders, insects, and snakes—all the strange and varied creations of the Earth—would be preserved on the lands set aside for bears. In a world where the rate of extinction is escalating rapidly and where ecosystems are disrupted long before they can be understood, it is essential that we safeguard portions of our remaining wilderness.

"Wilderness" is not, as the dictionary and our past practice both suggest, a synonym for "pathless waste." "Wilderness" is a verb. It is what the Earth does to create and sustain life on this planet, what it has been doing for the last 3.5 billion years, what we must hope it will continue to do for millions of years to come. In ways that are obvious, and others that are not, we need wilderness.

In an article entitled "The Ark of the Mind," Paul Shepard advances the idea that wildlife is, and always has been, essential to the growth of human consciousness. Our children, he suggests, turn to animals for their first lexicon of behaviors and attitudes (tail-wagging eagerness, purring contentment, chattering anxiety, growling ferocity). Our ancestors, for their part, looked to wildlife for insight into the fundamental mysteries of life: birth, puberty, healing, death, renewal. Today we too find ourselves moved by certain special animals, which retain the power to shape our awareness. Among these is the grizzly bear. By focusing our emotions, the grizzly permits us to understand and care about what is happening Out There and to begin to act.

"Artemis [the bear goddess] seems to beckon from the future, to call me toward who I am now to become," the Greek hero Hippolytus observed. She is also calling to us.

The Khutzeymateen Grizzly Bear Sanctuary was established in August 1994 as a joint project between the Province of British Columbia and the Tsimshian Nation. It is large enough to provide refuge for an estimated fifty grizzly bears. Not all stories have such a happy ending, however. In response to intensive lobbying from mining companies, plans to create a Southern Rocky Mountain Conservation Area to protect the Flathead Valley and its bears were put aside by the B.C. government in the late 1990s. An open-pit coal mine proposed for the Flathead Valley was shelved by the B.C. cabinet in 2004, but the area still lacks permanent protection.

SOURCES

The essays in this collection were written and published over a twenty-year period, as noted below. Magazine articles are reproduced here in full. Extracts from book-length treatments are excerpted from extended texts. For this edition, facts and figures have been revised, and stories have been updated wherever possible.

SURPRISING LIVES

"Parasites: Nature's Cling-Ons" originally appeared as "Nature's Cling-Ons," *Canadian Geographic,* March/April 1999, pp. 30–32.

"A Great Day for Grasshoppers: Outings in Entomology" originally appeared as "Peril of the Prairie?" *Canadian Geographic,* May/June 2002, pp. 44–50.

"Prairyerths: Entering the Underworld" originally appeared in *Prairie: A Natural History* (Vancouver: Greystone Books, 2004), pp. 92–98.

"Storm-Petrels: At Home with the Tubenoses" originally appeared in *The Wonder of Canadian Birds / Wings of the North* (Saskatoon,

Saskatchewan: Western Producer Prairie Books, 1985 /
Minneapolis: University of Minnesota Press, 1985), pp. 18–20.

UP CLOSE AND PERSONAL

"Mountain Lions: Seeing Ghosts" originally appeared in *Wild
Cats: Lynx, Bobcats, Mountain Lions* (Vancouver and Toronto:
Greystone Books, 1993 / San Francisco: Sierra Club Books,
1993), pp. 63–71.

"The Singing Forest: Diary of a Wilderness Canoe Trip" originally
appeared as "The Singing Forest," *Canadian Geographic,*
January/February 2004, pp. 36–46.

"Peregrine Falcons: Poisoned Prospects" originally appeared in
Peregrine Falcons (Vancouver: Greystone Books, 1992 / San Francisco: Sierra Club Books, 1993), pp. 7–10 and 95–103.

A FEAST OF FACTS

"The Nature of Wolves: Wild Lives" originally appeared in *The Nature of Wolves: An Intimate Portrait* (Vancouver: Greystone Books,
1996 / San Francisco: Sierra Club Books, 1996), pp. 31–44.

"Motherhood Issues: Mammals and the Maternal Instinct" originally
appeared in *Mother Nature: Animal Parents and Their Young* (Vancouver: Greystone Books, 1997 / San Francisco: Sierra Club
Books, 1997), pp. 31–39.

"Clever Corvids: A Mind for Food" originally appeared in *Bird
Brains: The Intelligence of Crows, Ravens, Magpies and Jays*
(Vancouver: Greystone Books, 1995 / San Francisco: Sierra Club
Books, 1995), pp. 92–104.

"Aurora Borealis: Airy Nothings" originally appeared in *Aurora: The
Mysterious Northern Lights* (Vancouver: Greystone Books, 1994 /
San Francisco: Sierra Club Books, 1994 / Toronto: Firefly Books,
2001), pp. 13–14 and 124–29.

HITS AND MISSES

"Skunked: Keeping Peace with the Neighbors" originally appeared
    as "Debunking the Skunk," *Canadian Geographic*, July/August
    1999, pp. 20–22.

"Saving Moose by Feeding Bears: Manna from Heaven" originally
    appeared as "Saving Moose by Feeding Bears," *Canadian
    Geographic,* May/June 1999, pp. 24–26.

"Rule of the Wolf: Restoring Order to Yellowstone National Park"
    originally appeared as "Rule of the Wolf," *Canadian Geographic,*
    September/October 2003, pp. 66–76.

"Caribou Stakes: Gambling for Arctic Oil" originally appeared
    as "Caribou Shuffle," *Canadian Geographic,* May/June 2001,
    pp. 30–36.

STAYING ALIVE

"Stuck on the Prairies: Where Is Here?" originally appeared in
    Prairie: A Natural History (Vancouver: Greystone Books, 2004),
    pp. 2–8 and 15–19.

"Urban Coyotes: The Trickster in Toronto" originally appeared as
    "Coyotes Colonize Toronto," *Canadian Geographic,* November/
    December 2000, pp. 34–36.

"Dances with Bison: The Wild and the Tame" originally appeared
    as "Back Home on the Range," *Canadian Geographic,* January/
    February 2005, pp. 50–60.

"A Future for Grizzlies: Artemis Beckons" originally appeared
    in *Grizzly Bears* (Vancouver: Greystone Books, 1990 / San
    Francisco: Sierra Club Books, 1990), pp. 3–9 and 115–19.

NOTES

The following books and articles are cited in this publication.

PEREGRINE FALCONS: Poisoned Prospects
Carson, Rachel. *Silent Spring.* New York: Crest Books, 1962.

THE NATURE OF WOLVES: Wild Lives
Murie, Adolph. *The Wolves of Mount McKinley.* 1941. Fauna of the
    National Parks of the United States, Fauna Series No. 5, 1971.

MOTHERHOOD ISSUES: Mammals and the Maternal Instinct
Ewer, R.F. *The Ethology of Mammals.* London: Logos, 1968.
Eyer, Diane E. *Mother-Infant Bonding: A Scientific Fiction.* New
    Haven: Yale University Press, 1992.

CLEVER CORVIDS: A Mind for Food
Bossema, I. "Jays and Oaks: An Eco-Ethological Study of a
    Symbiosis." *Behaviour* 70 (1979): 1–117.

Croze, Harvey J. "Searching Images in Carrion Crows." *Zeitschrift für Tierpsychologie Beiheft* 5 (1970): 1–85.

Zach, Reto. "Selection and Dropping of Whelks by Northwestern Crows." *Behaviour* 67 (1978): 134–48.

————. "Shell Dropping: Decision-Making and Optimal Foraging in Northwestern Crows." *Behaviour* 68 (1979): 106–17.

A FUTURE FOR GRIZZLIES: Artemis Beckons

Barbeau, M. "Bear Mother." *Journal of American Folklore* 59 (1946): 1–12.

Edsman, C.-M. "Bears." In *The Encyclopedia of Religion,* ed. Mircea Eliade, vol. 2, pp. 86–89. New York: Macmillan, 1987.

Shepard, Paul, and Barry Sanders. *The Sacred Paw: The Bear in Nature, Myth, and Literature.* New York: Viking-Penguin, 1985.

INDEX

KEITH BELL

*C*ANDACE SAVAGE is the author of more than twenty books, published over a twenty-five-year span, including thirteen on natural history and natural science. She has also contributed to *Canadian Geographic, Owl,* and other magazines. Her work has been honored by the American and Canadian Library Associations, Children's Literature Roundtable, National Magazine Awards, and Canadian Science Writers' Association, among others. In 1994, she was inducted into the Honor Roll of the Rachel Carson Institute, Chatham College, Pittsburgh. A frequent finalist for the Saskatchewan Book Awards, she has won the prizes for Children's Literature, Non-Fiction, and Book of the Year, the latter in 2004 for *Prairie: A Natural History.* Her next book, *Crows: Encounters With the Wise Guys of the Avian World,* will be published in the fall of 2005. She currently divides her time between homes in Eastend and Saskatoon, Saskatchewan.